ONE STORY
FOR ALL MAN

Jesse Antoine

McClain Printing Company
Parsons, WV
www.mcclainprinting.com
2010

International Standard Book Number 0-87012-795-0
Library of Congress Control Number 2010900868
Printed in the United States of America
Copyright © 2010 by Jesse Antoine
Wilmington, DE
All Rights Reserved
2010

CHAPTER 1

Millennia will pass and earth will still turn. This time, like the days after the dinosaurs, it will be quiet again - and we will be the fallen. But that's a long ways off, so for now, here I stand, where a breeze sweeps over my field, evenly and symmetrically holding its brown tips of grain sideways to the ground. I both saw and heard this, but felt nothing. But I was conquered by my impatience and in a moment I, too, was stroked by this breeze, simultaneously with the tree beside me. I looked up to observe his happy cavort and it made me smile, so I decided to sit beneath the jovial giant, letting my eyes gaze over the land that now descends at my feet.

As I sit with the pleasure of this moment by my side, I cannot help but to think back to a story of mine. It's a wonderful story which takes place over about one year. It's nearly entirely true. If I fib, you'll probably know it, because I'm not any good at it, so never mind. It'll take a lot of wind out of me, and some things won't be so easy to tell, so don't call me a liar, or I *will* stop now; I need not tell something flooded with fabrication when I have endeavored so diligently to seek my own truth. But I figure you know I'm going to tell it anyhow, so now that I've got you half-way stirred up, here it goes:

CHAPTER 2

I was sitting on a park bench just north of London; couldn't say where, for certain - now that I think of it. I had been sitting there for a considerable amount of time by now. There were some children playing nearby which I had the pleasure of observing. I even thought for a moment how fun it would be to join them, but swiftly declined the idea. So I continued to sit back in the most relaxed of states - ignorant of time. Down around my feet I noticed a line of ants marching intently to and fro an unknown destination around my bench. I watched them for a bit also - and with equal enjoyment. They maintained a perfect single-file line while carrying their goods back, I supposed, to home. But their route was grossly indirect around my bench, and so I discredited their race immensely. I alleged that they had all simply followed the first who found whatever food it was they were carrying.

With this slight disappointment, it seemed a good time to change atmosphere, but certainly not with any urgency – I'm not familiar with that word. So I pushed my hands against my knees and steadily made my way up with an old man grumble. I routinely stretched my back, then reached down and heaved my backpack onto my shoulders. Before my final departure, I glanced around once more as to give recognition to the place that granted me the simple pleasure of an enjoyable sit. The ants had once more caught my attention. When I looked at them, I caught a laugh from within; a single ant had deviated from that strict line of march, taking a short-cut home while carrying an enormous speck of food over his head. I had no one in the world to share it with, so it seemed my laugh would enter eternity unnoticed. I guess that was okay, though. As I walked away, I pondered on this ant: he may or may not find the best way home; but if he doesn't, he'll surely return having seen more than just the ant in front of him.

Whatever town it was, I was trying to get out of it; not for any particular reason - only because it was time to move. And there weren't any particular clock that dictated this movement, either - only my desire to see something different. The street that I moved into was a boring one; a residential with perfectly aligned trees trimming the street and perfectly white and wide sidewalks made for walking. I was told it was the main road out of town. There was an unlikely quietness from the absence of cars. Such an atmosphere permitted my focus to a diligent study of the well-kept and neatly kept houses that surrounded me.

Anyone that drove past me held their heads glued straight to the road as if I didn't exist. Finally a man in a black jaguar turned and looked in my direction, but kept-on past. Minutes later, still walking north, I noticed the same man driving the other direction, this time looking upon me intently – in the act of studying, which I briefly noted as a bit strange. Walking with my head down, which is typical of me, I looked up for the first time in nearly fifty steps and there was that black jaguar coming right toward me. My heart rate increased; a change I could clearly feel. The window came down and a completely bald man in his late thirties stared at me, but did not speak. I spoke first, 'The highway should be up here somewhere, right? - that's where I'm going.'

'Get in,' he said; nothing else. I hesitantly opened the door, put my pack between my legs, and sat down.

Now I must admit, American democracy is the best form of government man has ever known; where every man is created equal and I'll shoot whoever says otherwise. The Greeks and Romans were a good bunch too – thanks guys, for the idea. Yet, I'm glad we refrained from adopting several things quite so rampantly, although, I do suppose homosexuality has pretty well found its niche. And like I was taught, I'll have no parts of it and I'd prefer a society without, but straight from the words of the old Virginian aristocracy, and the rest who decided on a peoples' document, I guess they'll have their freedom too.

'So, where are you from?' he asked me.

He was gay; the gayest. Stunned and discomforted, I was only able to blurt out 'The States' for a reply, as my mind raced to think of a solution to this philosophically challenging situation. My prior experience with gayness in such close proximity was limited to none. All my life I was told of its evil, and so I came to steer clear of it as a personal choice as well. But I'd been walking for a while, and I badly wanted out of this town, so I hunkered tight and stiff in my seat as to go through with it. For a twenty minute ride I had my first conversation with a gay man. I was twenty one years old. I was very polite and even partly congenial to this man who drove past me several times checking for something. My destination arrived and I made my goodbye very brief and business-like. His eyes twinkled as a limp wrist flopped a very happy goodbye and it made me feel funny.

CHAPTER 3

It was overcast weather and nearing 6:00 pm if I recall correctly. There was a constant flow of traffic, while I stood aside watching. Most ignored my very existence as a fellow human being, keeping their eyes glued to the road they were driving on. A few would vaguely glance in my direction and do what quickly became my favorite: the toss-up of the two hands in the air as to indicate some form of helplessness or some sorrow for my very unfortunate state.

It was such a busy little road, this place. And because it was a round-about in design, there was no stopping, only a constant flood which directed two intersecting roads to north and southbound directions of a major highway. My pack grew heavy, so finally I set it down. For a moment, I grew into a weird state of humiliation -- as if they all knew one another and were conversing over the weirdo standing on the side of the road: "Why is the poor soul standing there? What is he doing? I wander what he wants?" I supposed they questioned. But I quickly overcame this feeling when I realized that everyone driving by was only seeing me for the first time and then gone. So the spectacle that I had contrived wasn't actually real.

Long after my interest in such matters faded, a simple cardboard sign reading NORTH still leaned upright against my pack as I wandered up and down the road to occupy time. I kicked some stones, but mostly threw them. My favorite is to aim at an exact point, especially metal, for hopes of a nice ping, in practice of my accuracy. I practiced for an hour, at least. Then I heard a loud set of brakes. A tractor trailer had stopped on the ramp that descended down to the highway about sixty yards from where I now sat. Was it for me? I couldn't be sure - those guys stop all the time for things. But a hand waving out the window indicated it was my ride, so I took off running full speed, sure not to miss it.

I came to the passenger door which was already swung open for me and there was a man waving me inside. The climb was much higher than I ever imagined and I had to throw my pack in first, which I almost immediately noted as a mistake. When I got in, I threw out my paw for a handshake and received a firm grip back.

"I'm headed to Scotland, where are you going?'

'Czech Republic'

Maybe he didn't understand. I'm almost positive you cannot drive to Czech Republic from England, and if you could, I hope that's not where we're going. He took off driving and again I sat stiff in my seat – quite nervous, but this time sure to be confident on the outside. The man beside me was in his forties, very large, fat, dark complexion, with deep blue eyes, big lips, unshaven for about six days on my scale, and generally someone I didn't think I should trust. I'm certainly not god, but oh yes, I judge. I skillfully determine the character of a person based solely on looks, and this man, I thought, was as greasy as he looked; skeletons behind the closet door, for certain – a murder, a rape, a drug problem; one of the big ones, I thought.

'My name is Jesse,' I said. And again, only 'Czech Republic' was the reply, as he gave an unhappy-seeming glance of the eyes and continued driving. This same reply immediately allowed me to understand both that he spoke little or no English *and* was quite uninterested in speaking with me. Well, I'll be damned, I thought – that's awfully snobby behavior – even if you are a murderer. Put me right in my place. I decided to stare out the window and didn't say another word. I never did catch the guy's name. I didn't know where he was headed, but I sure would have liked to known. I certainly wasn't asking for a map after I'd gotten such a rotten response out of an exchange of names. All I knew and all I cared about is that we were headed north. And as soon as he started to deviate from that direction, I was gettin' myself out of that truck one way or another.

We drove for two or three hours in complete silence. I still enjoyed myself like always. It takes a hell of a lot to damper me. Silence never did bother me much. I looked out the window and gathered on the new landscape I was witnessing for the very first time; I hadn't felt soil outside of the North American continent before this. Although my eyes were fixed to the landscape outside, you can bet I was watching and listening to every little movement this guy made. I was ready for anything.

For the first time in an hour, he deviated from his strict driving posture, reaching for something. I turned my attention and blatantly watched. Relieved that it was only a deck of playing cards, I immediately wondered what he had in mind. I acted casually uninterested in his actions, just to indicate that I was, indeed, minding my own business, as it seemed he wanted. Examining him from the corner of my eye, he fumbled with the cards some. One by one he went through each card eagerly while driving. Then a sound came from his voice which he directed at me. I'm sure it was something like "hey" in his language, but at the moment, it resonates only like that of a grunt. I looked and he was handing me a card. I grabbed it while studying his face in mid-grab, probably with a very speculative expression of my own. This was no regular playing card. Actually, it was a pornographic picture of a woman bent over. My facial expression was again, speculative, while my mouth couldn't help but crack a smile. I looked at him and he made a brief grunting laugh and smiled real big at me. I laughed back at him. Another card was passed to me and we repeated the smile – laugh – return laugh process. This went on through about one quarter of the deck, until, I suppose, his patience grew thin with this pleasure and we moved onto the next.

He was motioning for something by tapping on the seat between his legs. Mimicking him, I tapped on the seat between my legs, which, I think, came to strikingly resemble two cavemen in communication, supplementing language for grunts. A different pitch of grunt allowed me to figure out that he wanted something from under my seat. My blind hand felt only one hard object, and I pulled out a lap top computer. He set it on the dash, plugged it in, and slid in a compact disk that came from his sun visor. Considering the past half hour with him, I didn't begin take any guesses. I didn't need to, because an extraordinarily explicit video of Homer Simpson fornicating with Marge Simpson quickly took stage with a burst of unnecessarily loud laughter from Czech Republic which filled the truck cabin. I sat in complete silence contemplating the events upon me, while the laughter continued atop my thoughts. In an apparent disappointment of my reaction, the laughter simmered to a quick halt and now all silence was omnipotent but Marge's. When he reached to hit the next arrow on the computer, I wandered how much longer our porn experience together would last. And before I even finished pondering that question, Papa Smurf and Smurfette appeared on the screen doing the Dirty under a mushroom. This was followed by more prodigiously loud laughter and pointing, and I still didn't know what to think. Only because of the situation, not the movie, did I join in congruence with this man's laughter. Mine was more of an *oh my god this is crazy laugh*. I started low, then increased my laugh's intensity until we were both laughing louder and harder than ever. The more I laughed, the harder he laughed. And we watched several more movies together.

Not too long after our last movie ended, the truck made a sudden stop just before an exit. But he didn't take the exit; he only stopped on the highway shoulder and pointed to the road, pointed to the door, and then to the exit ramp. I guess this was my stop. I wouldn't have minded going a bit farther north with him, but I wasn't making the decisions. We were well into the countryside now. I waved goodbye as I lowered myself out of the truck and he didn't acknowledge me at all. I walked up a long exit ramp, eager to discover what was being held for me at the end. I'd say that's the primary motivation that brought me so far and long.

There was a small gas station with a country road stretching behind it, but nothing else. I got right to business, standing on the northbound ramp with my flimsy *NORTH* sign leaning on my bag. I was well-shaven, my clothes appeared clean, and my shirt was tucked in. The baseball cap probably screamed American, which, at the time, wasn't the most popular thing to be. I lifted my hat high above my forehead so the drivers could see my face. I looked at every passing driver directly in the eyes as to give them a momentary exchange of who I am. I only had a split second of this eye contact to convince them that I was honest and pure, so I used it wisely.

A vehicle passed about every seven minutes, which didn't quantify to my favor. After an hour or two, it started raining lightly and I wished my extraordinarily expensive poncho that I had purchased which was also intended to serve as a tent shelter, would not have fallen off the outside of my pack just before I climbed into that last truck. It was early May, but very chilly, and I was every bit of damp. As the rain came harder, I took my job as a hitchhiker more seriously, looking drivers dead in the eyes with a very pointy thumb. This continued for twenty rainy minutes, and the forest just behind me became increasingly appealing. Just as I was about to throw in the towel, pity became my favorite emotion as a man driving a luxurious bus assertively pointed at me as we met eyes, and pulled to the side.

'Where to?'

'I'm aiming for Edinburgh, Scotland, but anywhere north is good.'

'Well yey fer yew - Oy'm headed straight through Edinburgh,' came the reply in a Scottish accent so thick that I stood at the bus door still deciphering what he said.

'Ya coming or not? - bus leaves starting now, fella' he said in a tone so stern and serious that it reproached me a bit. I entered onto his steps with a hand out, saying 'Jesse,' and it was met with an even tighter grip than that of the man before. 'Bob,' he replied, and I took the seat directly behind him.

'Ya don't see people hitchhiking anymore now-a-days, well with the scum and that lot we didn't used to have. Ya . . .I spect' the world's a different place,' he ended in a discouraged tone. He was talking more to himself than me, I think. 'And I can't say I'm too keen on picking up bystanders in *my* bus, either, but I couldn't just pass up a man standing in the cold rain.'

'I appreciate it very much, sir,' I said in an attempt to show my best manners as to relax his nerves for having me on his bus.

We drove without speaking for a short while and I began rustling around in my pack. I saw Bob watching me in his mirror with a look of suspicion and he was noticeably as tense as I had been with Czech Republic. I retrieved a snack, which consisted of either cookies or crackers – can't recall. Being very hungry, I made myself at home, pulled down the tray and began my snack without considering my surroundings. As always, I was thinking of my manners and sure not to make a mess, but Bob swiftly intervened on my feast, commanding: 'You'd better not be making any messes on my bus, I just cleaned it. I keep a very clean bus and I don't want any messes.' It was clear now that I was under extreme scrutiny – suspect as potential scum. 'I'm making sure to be very clean, sir' I said loud and mannerly, making eye contact with him in his mirror.

Bob was in his late fifties. I determined he was a tough man and even at his age he could do some real damage. He had big strong hands and arms and a well-maintained body. I presume he assessed me in a similar manner - that's just what you do when faced with such an unusual situation as this. But when he realized he could half-way trust me and I wouldn't be any trouble, he relaxed his hard-liner attitude and we began small-talk. Naturally, he asked me little things, like why I was in the rain on the side of the road on the other side of the world; but mostly he began lecturing about things: government, society, changes in the world, his farm, and his services in the Scottish Guard. He didn't know a ton about the world and he admitted it, but he did know a great deal about his country, Scotland, which he loved with all his heart.

We made a stop for some late-night coffee and he wanted to sit down properly for the cup. We sat at a small, round table in a well-lit café at a rest stop. It was an awkward change in setting - you know, going from hours of conversation in a dark mirror, to finally staring each other straight in the face under bright lights. I'd left my bag on the bus which kept my senses set on sharp. I needed to use the bathroom and I was worried of letting the bag out of my sight for that brief stint of time, despite Bob seeming to be an upstanding and honorable man. But I couldn't afford to take chances – you must understand.

The conversation was clumsy at first, I believe, because of some cultural things, but mostly because of our huge difference in age. I was somewhat deficient in my man-to-man practice, but nonetheless, we discovered things in common and it quickly picked-up, and I got my practice. Here's what I remember:

'What do your folks think of you travellin' out here by yourself?'

'Can't say they're too pleased. Think I'm nuts, actually. They're fairly traditional
Americans and maybe don't believe so much in what I'm doing. They think I ought to be spending my time more wisely - making money and such.'

'Traditional, eh? Can't say I know what that means in America, but I'd guess it isn't hugely different than here. Traditional's aboot' the only good thing the world's got left. I can't hardly blame em'; I'd be worried for my boys out there too. Iteren't as it used to be. It just aren't safe – what yer doin', that is.'

'Ah, so I've been told many many times, Bob. But I think I'll manage it.' And that created a break in the conversation, so we sat in quiet a bit more, but not so uncomfortable like – just enjoying our cups. He finished his, so I offered: 'Would you like another, I'll get it for ya?' as to give my one dollar contribution to gas; in actuality, about all I could muster-up; I knew I had a very long road ahead. I didn't know where I was headed, nor how, nor when, however, the why was becoming all the more evincing.

He didn't take the second cup of coffee, but he did ask: 'Tell me, Jesse, what is your father like? I'll bet he's a damn proud man; man with a sturdy set on him - well judging by your undertakings, that is. Apple's never far from the tree.'

Actually, he and my father were exceptionally similar; in appearance and in actions, but I laughed and said 'I suppose that's pretty accurate - a tough working-man sort. One guy might do something tough, and he'd call it tough, but if I did the same thing he's likely just call it jackass. He says I owe him five hundred thousand dollars for my room and board, plus other luxuries he's supplied me with while raising me.' Bob revealed his ability to laugh, and it was quite a jolly laugh, which I liked coming from him, so I continued:

'All my life he said I could *do what I want when I got eighteen*. I got eighteen and I could *do what I want when I moved the hell out*. I moved the hell out and he's still the only man on earth that can make me feel like a child again. Oh, and I still owe him five hundred grand. I'd tell anyone - the president of the United States - how I felt about anything, and tell it with confidence, too. But somehow my opinion still feels downright boyish when I tell *him*, so I don't express it much around him anymore. But that's not to say he's not a good family man. I wasn't neglected or nothin'.'

He laughed, 'Sounds like my kind of fellow.' And then I knew Bob and I would get along just fine from here-on-out. Bob said I was a man in his book for going on such a journey and no one could ever take that away from me. He said my pop just loves me and wants to make sure I turn out alright, turn out tough, and not to be bothered by him. Our differences, despite being born and bred with such distance between, quickly diminished in light of our family similarities. He liked what I had to say. It even softened his firm military brown, which I never expected to happen when I first met him.

Out of earnest curiosity of Bob himself, I instigated discussion of politics. It seemed to be his favorite subject anyways. I questioned him on the nature of his government in relation to England's and general questions on the state of his country. He explained it all, and in the process, blew off some steam, I'd call it; but I think it was a pretty common release-valve of his. We were driving again – back to our mirror conversation. We talked into the night so much that I was eventually invited to sit in a pull-out seat right across from him for a more personal discourse.

'I used to love my country -- I love my country,' he said, 'but more than enough ails it, Jess. The English *still* want all the control – always moving in for more power and money. Hell, you know we've got cameras at intersections and on roads - deep in the countryside for Christ-sake? *"They're patrolling for speed. There are accidents out there,"* they say.' And he started getting angry with this: 'It's shite. Absolute shite! Let it burn for all I care. I only want to live in the country and be left alone with my family, but they've followed me there with their greed. And the people are asleep, Jess – they're dead asleep. They don't even realize what's happening right before their eyes. It's bad, I tell yeuh. We're headed for *noathin'* but trouble.'

I've had my own spell of anti-government sentiment, so I easily contributed to the conversation. I shared that we didn't yet have the problem with cameras, but I thought they could easily be there soon, however, if we ever did get them, I'd be the first of a thousand who'd shoot them down on the first dark night. But, in fact, I was being optimistic that others would join me; I wasn't completely convinced of my countrymen's will for freedom. But he liked it a lot, anyhow, so I continued the discussion: 'What we do have, however, is an abundance of overly powerful police that supply revenue by heckling the citizens under the disguise of traffic safety.'

'And the immigrants,' he said, '*holy shit.* They've come clear up to Scotland. Rightfully so, itisn't as bad as in London, but it's coamin'. I keep seein' it more and more up my way, and *one* is too many in my book. I feel like they're bloody rapin' my moather – raping my country plum dry. And we're simply lettin' them; and we keep lettin' em'… in by the thousands! – it's the Pakis' mostly, but no one seems to care that all these people who don't give a damn about the country – the country *my* ancestors died to make our own. It'll be the end of us. I swear by it. Keep your eyes on the teli, I'd make bet the whites'll be riotin' the streets of London before long. And it'll be bloody bad, too…'

He went on, and I tried to sympathize with him, saying: 'Three houses went for sale across the street from my family's house in a white neighborhood. Two were filled by separate families of some Arab sort and a household of fifteen Mexicans in the other. It made my father pace the floors.' This nabbed Bob's interest like I hadn't yet seen and he looked at me like he was surprised to hear me say it. To match him, I swore it'd be the end of America as well, which I may or may not have believed.

Bob was tired so we stopped for sleep. I was tired and happily agreed to this, although it was never an option, now that I think of it. When we woke, it was early morning. I was excited to see Scotland which Bob spoke so proudly of, at times. He was giving me the pleasure of a back-country entrance; no highway nonsense, he told me. He said when we get to the river and the big bridge, you'll know. He kept repeating this, because I kept reminding him not to let me pass it up. It was a grand entrance into Scotland with a personal coach bus-service and tour guide. Free of charge.

Bob treated me so kindly and we ended up getting along so well, that it was actually a sentimental departure. He felt the same, I'm sure. Our departure was graceful - men at their best. Bob liked me, I think, because I was a White Anglo-Saxon Protestant, and I liked him because he was honest and stood by his code of honor. He dropped me off just outside of Edinburgh, a big city, like he said he would. When the bus door opened, the bustling noises of a loud city struck the peaceful interior of the bus cabin with enormous disparity. It abruptly signaled the reality of our relationship's fate as forever terminated. We shook hands for an extended, but still short time, while he wished me to be safe, to keep my guard up, and to contact my father as much as I could. I thanked him for the kindness and goodwill that he showed, taking his advice with a nod. With one look, we both expressed a satisfied appreciation of our brief friendship, and I exited.

CHAPTER 4

Long after my short time with Bob had passed, and many days after I had explored Edinburgh, Scotland and many surrounding places, I found myself much farther North up the coast of Scotland in an extremely prestigious town called St. Andrews. The story I told of Bob may not have been of the greatest excitement, but it does, however small, play a part in this story that I am not yet entitled to explain.

St. Andrews was a quaint place. The weather was cold, but it didn't bother me none. Like all places I came to be, I endeavored to rid myself of tourists, or any area that contained an abundance of non-indigenous peoples. But great amounts of tourism wasn't something of consideration here, it seemed, so I enjoyed a walk and a sit for observation.

My American disposition generated countless discourses throughout my journey –many which began in dimly lit pubs in back alleys and side avenues in a search for local beer and people. The same stood in St. Andrews. After my sit, I moved to one of those dark pubs and sipped on a delicious ale. I'd been inadvertently hearing a conversation between two young men beside me. I suddenly became proud and inspired by what one of them said: 'No, you're absolutely right, *you don't hate anyone*. No matter who it is or what they are, you *just don't hate anyone*. Life's too short. There's no time for it.' In some variation or another, I had heard this before. I hope everyone has. I heard it from my mother and father, as well as their mother and father. In an instant, I was proud and inspired by my human race in their ability to liberate this idea through countless ages and ages – through mass migrations over the oceans, through time's of social and religious unrest and mass murdering, and through eras of great depression, poverty and hunger. I optimistically dreamed that the teaching had, indeed, transcended through time from our most ancient of ancestors, nestling its way into families all over the globe today – even in the most distant and obscure crevices and generations of the world.

With this feeling, I thought it was a good opportunity to interject. As my assumption went, it would reveal a strong connection between the two of us, and I leaned over to say, 'I'll bet you heard that from your mother, or maybe your grandmother, didn't ya?' in a cheery voice, to which a reply came: 'Actually, my mother died when I was young, and I never knew my grandmother,' only slightly turning his neck, barely paying any mind to me. I sat still, and only smiled inside at the likelihood of this reply as he turned away resuming conversation while I remained facing him in an engaging way. Some people might have felt awkwardly rejected - like an eighth grade boy at a dance, but I'm quite accustomed to this feeling from those dances, so it bothered me none. I almost never feel awkward; life's too short for that, too. Plus, I've been void of awkwardness ever since that day in ninth grade when I refused to stand for the morning Pledge of Allegiance, enduring through the first two commands from the teacher to rise, until my will was broken upon the third and I stood, only to reveal my enormous erection to a hysterical class whose attention was, of course, all on me.

I'm becoming familiar with English accents, and it's obvious that these two were at the top of the chain – England's best. They spoke like the queen herself – so proper, so eloquent. They could make most Americans sound like a buffoon with a few simple sentences. No sooner as I was appreciating this, did the other young man stand from his seat and approach me saying 'You will have to excuse my friend, he can be somewhat posh at times. I'm Emerson, pleasure to meet you,' and we shook hands.

'If I'm not mistaken, I *was* told by my mother -- *and* my grandmother, like you said, not to hate anyone, nor anything. You must have a good family. American, I presume?'

'How'd you know?'

'The hat, the sneakers, and the, what is it?' he read my shirt slowly, "*Easton Baseball*" T-shirt, to begin with.'

'And you're Scottish, I presume' I promptly shot back at him – knowing very well that he was English through and through. But he didn't catch my naughty joke, and properly corrected me: 'I'm English – somewhat of a difference' he said sarcastically. This spurred the other boy to join in laughing on Emerson's shoulder: 'Did he think you were Scottish, mate?!'

'Well, you are, too, aren't ya?' I asked.

'Ha! - my father would love that one, wouldn't he, Em?' nudging him with his elbow - which I didn't understand the relevance of until later. 'And he'll deserve another beer for it' said Emerson. 'Let's get this man more ale, can we?' he then demanded into thin air, which I was pleased with - as I didn't think I'd be affording myself another for that day.

Emerson and I went in and out of conversation due to the other young man's seeming requirement for exclusiveness with Emerson, which I only understood as a disdain for me. But he grew tiresome of our persistence and finally gave-in to a group conversation. We conversed on the normal introductory topics. I quickly learned of their superior class status, and didn't attempt to conceal anything about my own. They were more proper than I'd ever seen. I, a bit more crude and blunt than they had seen, which is why Emerson liked me -- for an interesting conversation piece, I guessed. I needn't speculate of their wealth, as the other one, Nathaniel, revealed it on his own. I was reminded of the great prestige of their University and the enormous intellect housed there; even the Prince of England himself attended, they casually boasted. Neither were they humble about their *own* intellect, which I could not disagree with by their obvious knowledge of many academic subjects, their oral eloquence, and a vocabulary that far surpassed my own.

But I evaluated that something was amiss. They appeared to be friends, but also rivals. Friendasaries, you might call it; secretly in competition to defeat the other. I regret to report the concluding generalization I would soon arrive at, that their intimacy with money had permeated the purity of their souls. And behind every poisoned soul is also a tainted mind - their intelligence, diluted. I won't go into explaining why I thought this, you'll just have to trust me on it, especially if this statement bothers you. Out of curiosity and a desire for companionship, I accepted an invite from Emerson to join them for dinner at a friend's place. I finished my beer and we walked to a flat where two girls awaited us.

It wasn't a far walk. Upon entrance, I noticed the dinner table was set for four. It did not seem a problem, however, and I was gladly accepted by the two girls. I noticed they were of a similar type to that of Nathaniel and Emerson, which is what brought the four together, I assumed. They proved to be an interesting company for me. I must now distinguish, however, the particular difference that I saw in Nathaniel from the rest. While I believed that they were all, to varying degrees, polluted by money, the others didn't have evil in them like he did. I'd hardly introduced myself to the friendly girls when I realized that my hygiene was seriously in question. Not so much out of self-consciousness, but in a swift consideration of the days ahead, did I openly ask:

'Do ya have a shower here?'

'Why, yes,' one answered speculatively.

'May I use it, please?' followed by a briefly stunned silence that prompted me to remind them 'It may be quite a while before I get to another shower. I hope they've told you of my means of travel.'

'Oh, yes, yes. Certainly, you may, Jesse' and I was escorted to the shower.

I took my pack into the showering room and went to work. The lack of obvious conversation outside the cheaply constructed door indicated they were talking about me. I paused a brief moment while undressing in the small bathroom to appreciate the situation at hand. I tend to study my present state of existence. Looking at myself in the mirror only further established my resolute tranquility and happiness, despite what may have been chatted about just outside the door. When I finished, I entered their parlor fresh and clean, well dressed, and closely shaven, and I suddenly became more appropriate for the situation. They were talking fine details of foreign politics, which I gladly listened to. It quickly shifted to American politics, which I found many Englishmen to be fervently interested in. I answered many questions. It was a serious and formal conversation; less relaxed than what I am accustomed to. I was not aware of how well old Nate and Emerson were acquainted with Julia and Sophie, but judging from the distance held, it was not an extremely secure relationship for the boys; they seemed to be on their best behavior. Dinner arrived at the table and I gobbled down my fruit salad topped with sun-flower seeds, followed by the main course of toasted squash, cucumbers, and tomatoes. When Nate and Emerson's avid wit momentarily resigned, I took the floor, asking 'So when's the meatloaf gonna be done?' and this made the girls, but not the boys laugh.

Somehow they got to discussing the topic of wit. The boys studied law and the girls, English literature.

'Those with the necessity to frequently engage in litigation are unquestionably obliged to have the most wit,' Emerson stated. But Sophie immediately retorted:

'Yes, while they may be obliged to *attempt* a demonstration of wit, as a student of literature, it is unlikely another study could truly enhance one's wit as does reading the words of our wittiest forefathers.'

'You may graze the greatest wit of the ages, but students of law are trained in Socratic Method, practiced in the true complexities of words, and tested on a whim. But I presume now you will request us establish a definition of wit,' Emerson politely spoke.

'Wit *can not* be taught, which is why the world is home to many horrible lawyers. Wit *can*, however, be better understood, and this is achieved by studying the best examples of it. The wit that you speak of, the on-the-spot sort, cannot be obtained from any education – it spontaneous nature can only be utilized by the equipment god inherently instilled in us.'

'Then I see you have not been educated on methods'
And this, I thought, terminally ended Emerson's chances with Sophie, because she didn't look happy.

'Excuse me?'

'Have you ever learned the proper way to do long multiplication?' Emerson asked with the sound of reason and explanation in his voice.

'Why yes, of course I have.'

'So can there not be such a method, also, to words?'

'Quite possibly, yes, however, not on a lawyers whim. Do you not sit with a piece of paper and pen to complete long multiplication?'

'Define the length of a whim.'

I thought she had a nice come-back. I enjoyed their little tiff, but to lighten things some, I rose from my seat and said 'I'm going to check on the meatloaf' and filled my glass with water. It didn't get any laughs this time, but I didn't care – I thought it was witty. As a good friend would do, Julie declared Sophie victorious in their battle for wit, and claimed students of literature the rulers of whit-on-a-whim.

'I didn't hear the definition still' Emerson desperately hung on.

What was this guy doing? Give it up, man – I thought, for the sake of the real victory you're after. Just then, Sophie openly suggested: 'Ten minutes.' Everyone including me was confused, but she continued: 'Everyone here gets a sheet of paper: law students, English students – even travelling hobo's,' she said - 'get's a piece of paper and has ten minutes to write the absolutely wittiest thing they can imagine. We'll judge when we are finished reading'

'We still haven't defined wit' said Emerson.

'Yea!' Nathaniel jumped in, 'Wit isn't something written on a piece of paper, it's the response someone can give to another. *And*, you two are trained in writing.'

'But you and Emerson are trained in long multiplication' Julie said.

Sophie contributed some more, ensuring that her little test would be completed by us all, saying 'What can be thought-of in a courtroom, can be thought of in this room, surely. Words are words, written or spoken. If you can think of them, as you claim you can, and on a whim, you can surely write them down. But just for you - to eliminate the definition of a whim completely, we have ten minutes.' She passed everyone a pen and paper, including me. I understood at least two people to be taking this seriously, and refusing to be a stupid American, it made three.

'So how do we judge it?' Nathaniel asked. Julie responded, 'I believe wit will judge itself. The final product will make itself obvious to us all.'

'Ten minutes - starting now.'

We all thought for some moments, then went to writing.

'Time is up.'

'You're up first,' Emerson put Sophie on the spot.

'Fine.'

And so she read:

'It is entitled:
<u>A letter to End a Love Affair</u>.
John. We cannot continue like this. My friends are getting suspicious and I found myself thinking if it's really worth it. Do you, John? I mean, you have your whole life ready - you've worked on it so hard. And I have my life still ahead of me; I am still able to become anything I want. And don't try to talk me over. I've decided. I've thought about all the nice days and nights we've spent together. All your funny jokes, little surprises and gifts you've done for me. It's really not you, it's me John. I just don't know if it's the right thing for me - that's all.

Actually... just fuck it. I changed my mind. Let's meet next Friday, okay?

Hugs & kisses,
Sandra'

We all laughed. 'Pure wit' Julie Proclaimed. 'I thought it was quite humorous' Emerson stated. I thought it was good, also. As the boys were both openly pursuing Sophie, I would give her even more points if it were designed as a message regarding her character, but I couldn't have been sure.
'Ladies first' Emerson looked at Julie. 'Okay' she delightfully smiled and began reading:
'Write now what I wish to say, what I want you to hear – that which is wholesome and true, this is my wit:
As intellects and attorneys go hand in hand, you must be great skeptics of the world. Herein lies my method: You will reject what you hear, and reason with what you say. This is good. At first reject everything - deny all. Then proceed to reason with the matters at hand and establish a truth. And when you establish that establishment, if you are truly reasonable, you will reason even more. And if you reason more, you should come to defy what you have first reasoned with and neglect what you have established, moving onto even higher enlightenment. So, naturally, at first, you should reject here what I say and ask, as you probably will. But do as you're told, fore I am the wit, the truth, and the light.

So as you were going to reject me because you think you know what you believe, reject instead, what you thought after that first establishment – that students' of law hold the wit, and accept what is true and reasonable. Accept rejecting your rejection of things for the wrong reasons. And now go; changed forever, denying all that you have believed but never truly reasoned with until now, you men of method.'

Not much was said, and so Emerson just read:

'Earth, or might I say Middle Earth – is certainly a place between two worlds; it is neither heaven nor hell, yet it breeds both life and death. We experience hell as witnesses to death, and feel heaven as we bear life.'

I hoped the brevity of this piece did not affect the magnitude of its wit, and I was prepared to engage my opinion, but, instead, said 'Your turn, *Nate*,' being the first to call him that, hoping to get under his skin a bit. So he conceded to read:

'Yes, I'll admit, she had a name. It was Charlotte. We had been together for nearly six months, and I've just recently lost her. You just know somehow, don't you? – when they're the right one; when they seem to fit so perfectly as you grip them tightly. She never fussed or complained – so complacent and content. I really thought I had her in my back pocket, but I must have been mistaken.
     The way she caressed my skin so smoothly…and wrote letters so passionately for me -how will a simple man like me proceed? It was the perfect relationship; utter harmonic concurrence. She just seemed to comply with my every move.
     -- That pen and my hand really had something special going. I guess I pushed her button too many times.
'Wait, Charlotte is a *pen*?' Sophie asked. 'Yes. I had a pen I was writing with for a long time, and I lost it the other day. I searched everywhere but couldn't find her. Irreplaceable, that thing - I loved writing with it. But it's your turn, now, *Yankee*. Let's see what you've got.'

And so I read:
'I learned things in school too, ya know?

Based on your socio-economic status, I can deduce that your behavior here takes root in a mutated Freudian-Nihilistic escape of the world, and its grossly enigmatically esoteric origin is a calamity of so long life. But you were probably right: all I know is that the world was created like this: There were a group of Hebrews. They did some fighting. Oh, and don't let me forget the Egyptians before that. Then there were the Greeks and Romans, and generally some powerful Italians for a good period of time after that. But suddenly these Vikings came down in the middle of all this and started burning shit. The Chinese might have been doing something over there by now, but who really knows - there's only one thing we can tell for certain - that the Africans are doing the same thing now since the beginning of time. Oddly enough, those Vikings came back in the form of Nazis to burn more things. But luckily a place called America came along and obtained some really big guns and decided everyone needed to relax. Now they're trying to govern the world - and they're led by the Vikings, funded by the Hebrews, soldiered by the blacks, and fed by the Mexicans.'

CHAPTER 5

Every day that I wake is more enlightening than the previous. I am free now – more free than I have ever been. Any direction I choose to take is the direction I go. For the first time I have no obligation to take out the trash, do the dishes, listen to a boss, a teacher, or a coach. My free will is all that reigns now. As a result, my spirit is greater than I have ever previously experienced. I am no longer contained in the cages of plastic cell phones or between the bars of four-lane traffic. The simplest pleasures are my greatest companions. I attribute much of this to time – my total disregard for it, that is. I think animals are averse to time, and so now I join them.

I utilized my cardboard north sign as much as I could, letting it take me to the farthest reaches of Scotland into the Arctic Circle where I was alone on a most desolate planet; a scary reality when I took a moment to considered it. At some point, I was inclined to ask Nathaniel "If you were the king of your own castle, what would you be like?" and only that, we'll say, ended my stay there. Now in the barren hills of the highlands, there are no laws restricting my travel to highway exits and off-ramps. I'm beginning to *really* use my legs. I was irritated by the scarcity of cars in other places before this, but now I see that impatience was a silly emotion.

As a good listener of my story you should be wondering by now if I have a goal of any sort, because surely no good story is without a main goal. But you're listening to a goalless story, so pay close attention.

As the nights got colder the farther north I travelled, everything became scarcer: cars, woods…trees, people, barns, food, and so I am forced to consider strategizing certain things for my own safety. I had explained my situation to many people on their way north: "I'm a travelling American student. I'm just looking for proper room and board for the night. Would your barn possibly be available?" And wouldn't you know, when I'd just come right out and say it, I was never once denied a night's sleep in a barn all throughout Europe. Many times, in fact, I was welcomed inside the home – with family, children, food and all. Despite all other events that might happen from here-on-out, my one and only final report is of the gentle kindness of humanity everywhere. And despite witnessing mans stringent dedication to laborious and monotonous daily occupations, the human spirit remains content and joyful so long as bellies stay filled with food; a meager request.

However great my spirit was, it became devastatingly broken in a matter of nights in such a rugged terrain. I learned quickly why people did not occupy this beautiful land the first night I woke up with thousands of tiny bugs crawling all over my body. Midges, they called them, and they were an unstoppable force; one which forced me to move south immediately – now with a ferocious sense of time, travelling day and night. My new course led me along the opposite, West Coast of Scotland.

I began thinking of Ireland. I'd been inquiring to many folks how I might best get there. One afternoon after many hours of walking, I was hungry and stopped at the only place I'd seen all day: a stone house that stood alone on a far-reaching hillside along the ocean. While eating a bowl of soup, I stumbled upon a conversation with an old-time sailor who claimed he often made this trip to Ireland in a boat. His grey beard and knitted hat indicated he wasn't telling fibs; mine indicated I was just American and homeless. After some smooth-talking, which, I became pretty good at, I scored a night's sleep and a promise for Ireland.

Innes was his name, and I could barely understand him. The language barrier was far worse than Bob. Each sentence was like deciphering code with English embedded somewhere deep within. I figure he was older than seventy but younger than eighty. After a straight whiskey together, he drove us to his home roughly ten miles away on a mess of lonely back roads. I wasn't familiar with the make of his car. It was a rusty, white compact-car with a standard transmission. He rambled-on quickly about some things, only a quarter of which I understood, and anytime I interjected, he'd come to a sudden pause, slightly tilt his head back, and look over at me sharply from the corner of his eye -- very much like you might expect a pirate to behave. After the sharp look, he would laugh with a few quick and hard chuckles and continue on rambling. He was quite funny and I enjoyed him right away. Innes was the epitome of cool.

As we entered the gravel driveway, his house was visible atop the hillside. We were in an equally rural area as the soup joint. Innes told me he built the house himself a very long time ago. The cottage walls were made of stone and it had a straw roof. Just then I remember catching a glimpse of his gnarled knuckles; one hand rested on the steering wheel, the other on the shifter, and I was able to visualize the ware and tear this job had caused on his body. My eyes moved upward to his once pale face, and I noticed his full lips escaping the white beard as they were about to speak. We breeched the peak of the hill and behind the house was an endless range of hills where sheep freely roamed. No other houses were in sight.

Innes' wife stood in the kitchen area as we entered. She was a proud and honorable woman; I could tell immediately from looking at her. Before she spoke, her eyes and smile allowed me to see the kindness in her heart; genuine love emanated from this woman. It looked liked she was wearing hand-knitted clothing. She wore a white top and a skirt made of pretty blues that went to the ankles. We were introduced and she embraced me with a motherly hug. I received it with great pleasure, because I felt in desperate need of her motherly offerings.

It was late evening by now and the sun was near closing time. Innes began pouring us glasses of whiskey and escorted me outside to wander about the house and the property for a while. By way of deciphering code, I was trying to establish some definite plans for our trip to Ireland, which, naturally, concerned me. I didn't know if he was a crazy drunk, or a madman ---- no wait, actually, I did – but that's what I loved about him. But if he did have a boat, did he really know how to navigate all the way to Ireland? How far was that? I had no map to even tell me where I was at the moment of drinking whiskeys into the night, and it didn't look like I was getting my hands on one before we left, either. He seemed totally unconcerned, and told me not to worry – assuring me I would be in Ireland before I knew it. I remember having some bread late at night, then being escorted to my cot, which quaintly rested in the living-room quarters, freshly made with hand knitted quilts and a fluffy pillow on top. The living room was connected with the kitchen area. The only other room was their bedroom, which was behind a closed door. I felt especially safe here, so considering that and the whiskey, I recall falling asleep immediately.

My wake-up call came earlier than expected, as I noticed that it was still dark outside. I couldn't have slept more than four hours. I was groggy from the drinks, but a large cup of strong, black tea, a bland porridge, and the notion that I would be sailing to Ireland with a drunken old man in who-knows-what kind of vessel stimulated my wits just fine. Innes asked me what I had to wear and I pulled out a cotton hooded sweatshirt, and some other lightweight cotton T-shirts, which he declared to be "no good shite" and accommodated me with a heavy black wool sweater and hat. He packed a sack full of hard bread and two jugs of whiskey and a small metal tool box of some sort. The car ride was farther south on the coastline than I had yet seen, but not more than a thirty minute drive. We parked along the water on a rocky bank near several houses. Floating in the water were several sailing vessels that I could barely make out for lack of light. I was instructed to stay in the car as Innes slammed the door and walked quickly to one of the houses. He returned minutes later with another older man and we unloaded the car to a nearby dock and were ferried by a small aluminum boat out to our sailing vessel. They spoke a little on the walk to the dock, but it was Celtic and I couldn't understand. I was never introduced to this third man.

We jumped aboard our vessel and Innes made a goodbye salutation to him that I didn't catch either. So there I stood: I hardly knew this man, I was lost and alone in the world, and I was about to sail the open ocean in an old, and what seemed to be, poorly maintained boat. But I was offered a swig of whiskey from the jug because I apparently looked tense, so I accepted. After the small, unidentified black outboard engine puffed to a start, we headed out of our cove toward a loch that opened to the Atlantic Ocean. There was a fair amount of wind, but the water in the loch was calm. I don't remember the name of the loch, exactly, but I do recall the name of one town I'd passed two days before: *Mallaig*, I think it was spelled. So I was somewhere south of there, for certain.

After five or six more passes of the jug, I didn't care where I was, I was just enjoying the bow of the boat and the breeze in my face. That breeze grew stronger the closer we came to the ocean and the further we retreated from the calm seclusion of the encompassing mountains of the loch. As we cornered the last mountain, the breeze grew to an intimidating gust. I didn't need to be reminded when we got to the ocean that "We're ent'ring the ocean!"-- but I was anyhow. The changes were obvious: the water went from calm to choppy and we were penetrating a clear break in the mountains on our left and right, heading straight into open waters of the Atlantic.

Our vessel was probably thirty feet long with chipping white paint, salt-worn masts, and a drunken captain and first mate. We headed into the dim waters with only the slight opening light of morning at our backs. After we cleared the last of the mountains and, I think, formally entered the ocean, we passed one island on our left that was about a mile out, then more islands in front and to our right another mile onto that. When we reached those out to our right, Inness shut the engine off. He lit a cigar and stood with a serious look as he puffed a few times studying into the water. When he started unwinding ropes and turning cranks, I was asked to get behind the wheel and steer us "that way," as he pointed.

In no time, with one single burst of an opening sail, I felt movement that steadily gathered into legitimate *speed*. This was my first ever feeling of being propelled by the wind. It was fantastic; amazingly natural and curiously unnatural. Another sail blew open and we gained more momentum through the water. We reached what seemed to be optimum speed and Innes laughed to himself as he stood to the front of the boat holding his jar of whiskey in the air as a gesture back at me. The swells were pretty big and a wave splashed in from the right side of our boat just at that celebrated moment.

All day we stayed just within visibility of the shoreline. There was a steady, strong, wind, and we kept a mighty pace. I stood with my two feet planted firm to the ground, with my chin up, tightening all of my muscles, and embracing the thick, powerful wind. I felt as though I were in the midst of fulfilling some long-lost Viking roots. The air was cold and my right side was scattered with wetness from sprays of ocean water. My ears were consumed with the incessant sound of wind -- soothing to a Viking. Without uncertainty, I belonged. Looking at Innes and his prominent jawline behind that healthy beard as he stood on the other end the vessel felt like I was amongst ancient kinfolk.

The jug was placed back into my gut like the handoff of a pigskin football, I sipped, then exhaled a small pocket of air and tightened my gut and throat as it went down. The waves were assuming their direction at a perfect ninety degrees to our boat, which made us fluidly glide over the water – much less impeding than a head-on approach. But the farther we went out, the bigger they got and I was concerned for the Wooly Mammoth - the name of our boat. Dark and thick puffy clouds moved overhead as the day went on, but the rain held off. I became seasick – taken by a terrible greening dizziness, similar to the one smoking cigars gives. I tried to put my head down to hide from the misery, but Innes growled and gritted his teeth at me with instructions to "Wake up! – don't take your eyes off that horizon. Fight it! If you're strong enough, it will pass." I did what he said, and within two hours of diligent concentration on the horizon, I slowly gained ground on the sickness until I ultimately brought myself to a valiant victory of wellness, inspired by the angry commands of my captain. This made me feel even stronger, and more like I belonged.

We alternated steering, but Innes always directed where to go. 'I've been sailing these waters for 60 years' he said slowly in thick dialect. 'My grandfather first took me out. I miss that man something dear.' He stopped to think a while. 'But now I'm the old one, and afraid of nothing,' which was obvious, but not at all disconcerting: for I was so free and in a place that may be my fatherland.

Actually, it was just the whiskey talking. As night came, the strong wind faltered a bit, but did not cease. The moon was bright and made the thick clouds translucent. When I looked to the sky, it appeared I was in an old black and white Hitchcock film. Toward land was a darker shade of darkness. I was very tired from a weathering day. Innes suggested: 'Go beneath and take your rest. You'll be needin' it in the days coomin.' The Irish are a funny bunch. Youghta pay close attention and not be troostin' a soul.'

'Like I did you, ya mean?'

'That'd be right. But you've got good sense, I know it – you knew I weren't no harm to ya.'

'I knew,' I returned sincerely.

So I went below. I twisted and turned for a while, despite being in a perfect state for sleep. Anxiety overcomes anything, I guess. My sickness gained ground on me as I lay horizontal on the bed. I may have slept two hours or slightly more until I was woken by Innes calling from the hatch just above. I sluggishly arose from my bed - could have been the whiskey, but, no matter, I knew what it was time to do. Again, I would have to leave someone whom I allowed myself to trust, which never came easier to me. I'm sentimental I suppose. It was still night when I went above. I saw that we were entering a cove. The faint moonlight revealed the silhouette of a steep cliff to my left. We were running on engine now, but he soon cut it and we drifted, rocking left and right into a complete stop. Waves crashed on the rocks to our right, which increased the intensity of the situation just enough to put me on edge.

'This is it, my friend' he said. 'Can't say exactly where ye are, but on the north side of Ireland, that's for certain.'

'I'm getting out here?' I looked into the water.

'You've got a better place?' he asked smartly, like a wise old man should.

'No, no. It's good.'

'I'm sorry, you'll have to get a little wet, but I gather you'll survive from it'

'Indeed, I will,' I smiled, then looked down to my feet, humbled by all his generosity. Then I shook his rough, old hand. We looked each other in the eye for an extended period - both smiling. It was another goodbye I can never forget. Nothing more was said; I just turned and jumped into the water with my pack overhead. It was nearly up to my waste. I didn't look back until the engine started again, and when it did, I realized about the sweater and hat.

'Your sweater!' I yelled sort of hesitantly, for fear of disturbing the perfect and unknown quiet behind me.

'Scotland's gift, ma friend!' and so the sweater sits within a chest drawer, just through the woods from where I now sit telling this story, inside a 100 year old farm house, on a mountainside that resembles those around Innes' house. Makes me happy to remember on such things.

CHAPTER 6

I wasn't going to tell that last story but I thought, hell, it's a good one, I'd better not skip it. So I'd sailed from Scotland to Ireland and never paid a single dime. I would have swam if it saved me a dollar. I was intent on having food in the scheme of my near future.

So I came ashore all wet and naturally the first thing I did was change my britches. I put on a dry pair of pants, and sorry I call it that, I know there ain't but one of it, but I got to walking through, I guess you would call it a town, and before I knew it, I was damn near on the other side of the country. Innes had let me loose somewhere in the northernmost tip of Ireland just as he said he would. I traipsed all through Ireland, beginning with Belfast, then down to Dublin, then further along that coast into Cork, which is where this next story begins, and really, where the meat of this whole thing starts taking place.

I never stayed in them big cities more than one night. Couldn't stand for, at the time, what was an eleven Dollar beer in downtown Dublin, so I quickly moved my beer-drinkin' elsewhere. They were much cheaper in, what I'd call a big town, named Cork, but it was the third largest city they had – or so someone said. I found myself far too many beers deep one night and without a roof over my head. It was real late by now and only the real crazies were those remaining. The sidewalk was overcrowded with drunks, which rightly included me. I was regretful for getting so bad-off in the interest of keeping on my toes and not allowing anyone to sneak me or hurt me in any way.

I'd talked to a lot of folks that night, which was enjoyable, but I needed rest; the road behind me wasn't easy and that before me would prove to be much more difficult. I stumbled around and landed in an area much less crowded so I could have some sleep, at least I figure that's what I did. Before I knew it, daylight was up and there I was lying on the concrete cuddling up with my bag like it was a plump woman keeping me warm on a cold winters' night. People were already bustling themselves off to work, walking right by my head. I fought-off the sunshine glaring at my eyes through two buildings across the road. I tried to ignore the combination of the two and sleep more, but it didn't work. I was awake with my eyes closed while my mind was working out an arrangement to where it would tell my body to stand up and move. When I heard a strangely twisted Irish accent around the corner, my attention was momentarily diverted from this nonsense of standing up. I gave the voice special recognition as strange, and waited for it again with my eyes remaining closed as a shield from the light. When it returned – I detected an even heavier twang. It was close enough now that I could make out the words:

'Does anyone hea' know how I can geet ta Deengle?'

The town is actually spelled Dingle, but the man had a thick Australian accent. I had crossed this place earlier somewhere on a map and it looked like an interesting area I might go visit. I knew it would be a difficult trek, though; such a place so far into the countryside could take a year by way of hitchhiking. I was still tired from countryside hitchhiking in Scotland because it consumed such a great amount of time. It was unlike me typically, but somewhat fitting of a street bum, when I loudly yelled to him just after he posed this question:

'How ya gettin' there!?'

My eyes opened halfway after I said it and a man walked around the corner and looked down at me. He studied for a minute, then said 'Well Oi've got me a ca' reented, whuy?' with an extra bit of wind in his 'wh.'

'Because I thought I'd like to go there myself, can I come with ya?'

He paused for a good twenty seconds, then said 'I don't know exactly where I'm going or what I'm doing, and I don't even know for sure if I'm going,' he babbled on some stuff that didn't affect my determination whatsoever.

'Ah, come on. I don't care where ya go, I just want to get out of here. I'll give ya what I can for gas. I'm an American student – just got stranded last night – you can trust me,' I tried to explain 'I'm studying to become an English teacher. They let me work with children.'

He thought even more this time, and stuttered out some groans and mumbles, but finally said very slowly, 'Well…I reckon… if you want to split gas with me…'

'Great, when would you like to leave?'

'Well, Oi'd loyk to check out thees hea' town a beet fi'st' he said.

Then I hopped to my feet, shook my head left and right to wake myself up, and confronted him with my hand for a shake. 'Jesse.'

'James,' he returned.

'Shall we walk the town together?'

'Su'a, mate.'

We walked around a short while. He was a very anxious and impatient seeming guy. He walked fast to the end of the cobblestone streets as if each one were his final destination. Then he would look left and right and quickly choose his next direction. My pack was with me, so my shoulders weighed heavy during the walk. It didn't take long before he said he wanted to go, which I thought was a great idea. James was in his fifties. He wore a ball cap and large sporty sunglasses. He had big lips and rough skin like an alligator, and a scar across one of his cheeks. He looked at me very strangely and something warned me not to trust him, so I didn't. It wasn't the scar.

He asked me to stay put while he checked out of his hotel, and he would bring the car along, so I did. I didn't know if he would come back or not. I was sure this was his way of escaping his newly acquired partnership. However, I sat there with extreme patience – I wasn't worried about it in the least. I was on a bench, not directly under, but beside a massive oak tree where there was a stone building just down a brief hill and across a small cobblestone road. A little girl stood in front of the building beside her mother. She stood as still and patiently as I, while her mother spoke business with a gentleman on the corner. The girl had fair skin and pretty strawberry blonde hair. Seven, I would guess. I observed her fine patience. She studied the ground, she watched people walking by – a very observant little thing for that age. Nothing within sight got past her, it seemed, except me.

Then, all at once, the whole town of Cork was swept by a great gust of wind. Leaves tumbled and skipped down the sidewalk and swirled up against the corner of the stone building into a whirlwind tornado. I saw it first, then right away glanced at the little girl who looked directly at me and smiled, then bolted from her mother's side to catch the rare phenomenon before it ended forever. Running at full speed, she ended with a two-footed stomp right in the middle of it. I watched the leaves and dust circle around her while she spread her arms out and tilted her head back, looking right into the blue sky. She rotated her body toward me so that I could see her smiling as big as she could. The bold red lips tightly pulled up on each side without showing teeth. My face went into a humbled expression as I watched, then James pulled up in the car.

The countryside came quickly. I was trying to feel this guy out. Something felt wrong – he was jumpy and very… sort of, lookative - to best describe it. We asked about each other's backgrounds. He was travelling the world by way of rented car.

'Don't you have any family or a wife back in Australia?'

'Nah. Had me a gealfriend, but she broke up with me lost month. Had some money stashed away, so I decided I'd head out - see the waerld.'

He indicated he wanted to stop in several towns on our way to Dingle. I conveniently agreed to anything: 'That's okay, so do I. I'm along for the ride, James.' But I asked him if we could go to a grocery store for some food before we left Cork. He agreed.

So we began to stop in small towns all along the way. All of the towns grew strangely similar; so much so that they gave us a terrible case of the creeps. *Ireland*, in general, started to get very weird – the people in the back hills, mostly. It's like the country of the elves - a different genus of white man. And since every town looks exactly the same, it's difficult to recall exactly which one I may have been in at any given part of this here story. It was a real life trip to The Twilight Zone: the countless avenues of connecting homes on cobblestone road - all painted of the same quirky pastel blues, greens, yellows, and whites.

We weren't really stopping for anything specific, just to stroll around and have a look. Some towns were flooded with tourists, which James liked more than I, but would quickly change his mind when he walked the streets amongst all of them, often suggesting a sudden divergent such as getting a drink at a bar. While walking in one particular town, we passed shoulder to shoulder foot-traffic on a wide sidewalk. The masses of people came in both directions, but without order whatsoever. Walking behind and to the left of James, I brushed right against a man who has not left my memory since the day. I recall this moment, as well as all future encounters with him, with a strangely vivid recording in the mind: time itself seemed to be slowed, not only in my memory, but in real-life, despite each encounter with him being merely seconds of time.

As he approached me amongst the massive crowd, I noticed him at about five feet out. James' attention was completely occupied elsewhere; I took positive note of this. As he gained the proximity of five feet, we met eyes and they were sustained in meeting until he completely passed – each of us turning our necks beyond ninety degrees of our shoulders. He was a tall old man - maybe 65, but not frail or weak – instead, strong and powerful. He had white, slicked-back hair, broad shoulders, with a slender build. His nose was pronounced and face chiseled and defined. I looked into his eyes, which were of the palest blue imaginable. He wore a trim black leather jacket. It was hot out. For reasons I will later reveal, in this split second, the feeling of severe fright consumed me utterly and entirely. It moved up from my spine and raised the hair on the lower back of my head. All this happened in the middle of the day with the sun shining bright. In that moment, I felt the presence of evil like I have never before experienced.

We moved further south following this event, which, actually, was only an event to me - and no one else on earth. The countryside became more prevalent the more we traveled. Each time we exited the car, I never left James out of my sight. My pack – my lifeline – depended on me to keep it safe. James suggested we begin searching for a cheap place to sleep. I hadn't showered or slept properly for some time, so I agreed to it. We split a cheap room. The next morning we got hold of a map and executed a better plan: we would drive the entire southern coast of Ireland together, including all four peninsulas, then halfway up the west coast where we would part ways in Galway. He would then head north to where I'd already been, and I'd head east in search of a boat to mainland Europe: France, that is. We travelled together for the next fifteen days. But for now we were wondering how to exit this town and James inquired to the first guy that walked by.

The man he chose thought for a second then said, 'I go. I go vees you,' in broken English. James and I looked at each other, and mutually consented, without saying anything. He was a shorter sort of man, but very muscular, with jet black hair, and extremely white teeth -- probably twenty five years old. He wore a funny Lenin Eastern European shirt that exposed his chest. Around his neck hung a large bear claw. He immediately sifted through his backpack and extracted topographical maps of Ireland and began pointing to many areas, suggesting we visit. He seemed to know some interesting things that we didn't, so we both welcomed his company. We drove endlessly along an uninhabited land. I sat in the front seat of our white, compact car, while James drove, and the even stranger Kamile sat behind me during many days of travel. He never spoke much, unless it was a demand for us to take a particular direction.

We drove ten hours in search of the first set of ruins that Kamile indicated he knew of from the map. I was excited to see the pagan, star-mapping rocks, and despite getting lost many times over, we continued searching. Eventually it seemed we needed to park the car and walk. Miles up a mountain and through sheep-grazing fields, we finally found the puny waist-high stones pointing to the sky. We each guessed what they were built for. I called them maps of the stars, James said they were religious places, and Kamile suggested intently that we were both stupid and wrong: "eet ees joost a ba-b-q." We slept there that night under the stars. I couldn't get the stone map to line up with anything.

After climbing many of the largest peaks in Ireland, wandering into forests and up mysterious streams, and in search of more ruins that Kamile guided us to, we made it to the town of Dingle in about a week. It was clear at the end of a long peninsula of the Irish island, which took a lot of effort to get to - considering the roads wind every thirty yards consistently over there. We all laughed at the Irish for being such a backward group of people. Several times, we took pictures of the speed limit saying 70 km/hr in one direction and as we looked behind us, it said 50km/hr going the opposite direction. And we got lost many times, but not because it was our fault. We came to a fork, and we knew which road we wanted to take, but their signs, I swear by the lord, pointed directly in between the two roads a solid fifty percent of the time. James told me the Australians have jokes about how the Irish are dimwitted, but I never heard of such a thing. We only had Polish jokes that I knew of, and he had never heard of those. This, for once, sparked Kamile to speak, because he was Polish. Otherwise, he had no real interest in speaking to me, and only a bit to James.

Together, we got out and walked the town of Dingle. Mutually, we commented how the town was spooky like the rest, but worse because it was deserted entirely - hardly a soul in sight. We went into some shops and the people tending them all looked upon us very strangely. There were small avenues that wound up hills and twisted and turned. We were walking fast, searching for something - can't remember what. I remember waiting outside of a gift shop while James purchased something. Kamile had disappeared. Not far down the hill, I observed a man walking across the street with his hands in his pockets. Moments before he disappeared behind a building, he turned and looked directly at me. I immediately recognized him, and could only think the words "Oh, my god" to myself. We had travelled so far away from where I had last seen him in that crowd of people. It seemed impossible, but I was certain it was him. It frightened me terribly. I tried to find a coincidence that simply wasn't there. Could he be following me? Am I going crazy? - I don't know. James came out the shop door which rung a bell, and said: "Mate, let's geet the heell outta hea', this place geaves me tha creeps." I didn't ask why. We just left in a hurry.

CHAPTER 7

Kamile was more like a predatorial animal than a man. He licked his lips a lot and stared at things like a cat. When he saw something out the window he liked, he was impulsive and required us to stop at his command. He laughed at things that seemed very normal to the rest of us. And when he laughed, he stuck his pointy tongue completely out and lowered his chin closer toward his chest, showing his top row of extra white teeth. He was very much like a cat, actually: inattentive to human speech. When we let him out of the car, sometimes he would take off running up a hill or into a forest and we never knew what he was going after. James still kept his distance from me, as did I from him. But it was casual, not bad; our partnership was based on business more so than friendship. I was fine with that. He didn't seem to trust me and nor did I trust him entirely. When we stopped for hikes or walks, we wandered off in our own directions.

When we finally found Kamile in Dingle, he was standing on a street corner staring at the sky as if he had never seen it before. We grabbed him and immediately left. We traveled along breathtaking coastal roads as we moved north from the bottom of the large peninsula. There were hardly any inhabitants in the region. We kept a fast pace in that little car, screeching the tires through every ocean-side turn with a cliff beneath. When the ocean left our sight, we were really in sheep territory, and that's when Kamile began to bang on the window. James looked back at him and asked 'Well what do you want, mate?'

'Stop' he demanded.

'Stop? You con't be serious.'

'Stop.'

We stopped. Kamile exited the car, taking his military looking pack with him.

'I leave now' he said.

'You'll do *what*?' James asked. 'Kamile, we'a in the meadle of no whe'a!' he said as if Kamile understood – I had trouble myself sometimes.

Kamile only said 'We are finished. Goodbye,' and he turned around and started walking. But he hardly got five feet and turned

43

back around and said 'Whoa, whoa, whoa,' and started laughing with his tongue out 'one minute!' and he fumbled around in his military-looking pack, then pulled something out and handed it to me. 'You would like zees?' he asked me through the window, giving me some papers. I grabbed them and he only said 'Czech Republic.' It was an airline ticket to the Czech Republic. He never shook hands, just took-off running up the steep side of a rocky mountain. There were no towns even remotely nearby; no roads in the direction he walked for sixty miles; and certainly no people.

James and I drove some more that evening, but the day grew thin soon enough, and when night arrived, we began searching for a good turnoff to park the car and sleep. When we found the perfect spot, we were surrounded by a tall forest on all sides and it was pitch-black outside of the car. There were few signs of civilization. We hadn't seen a house for miles. As soon as the ignition cut off, there was a stagnant silence inside the little cabin as the overhead light dimmed until we couldn't see. Yet, after a ten hour day of riding, we were far too tired to be concerned and immediately reclined our seats as far as they would go and tried for our sleep. But it was stuffy and we had to crack the windows for ventilation. The crickets were loud outside; loud to the point of disturbing. Right away, my body told me I needed to go for a piss, so I told James what I was doing and exited the car. Standing at the trunk, I looked into the forest, which was very black. I looked up and could see deep into the universe of stars. My stream was flowing. Then I heard it. I thought I was imagining something at first, but yes….the more I listened, the clearer it became. It was coming toward me. I stared into the forest edge, which was some twenty yards away. Someone, just inside the tree line was playing the flute.

'Jesse?' I heard James ask from inside the cracked window of the car - reminding me that I stood alone out there. I looked for anything moving as though my life depended on it. But it was far too dark to make anything out. I was absolutely terrified for the third time in a week. I felt the hair lifting on my arms. I suppose you know exactly who I thought of. I went to the car and closed the door firmly shut behind me. The interior light dimmed to nothing and James and I sat together in the dark. I couldn't see his face but he was right next to me.

'Jesse,' he said so very slowly with a concerned tone '*Tell me* that was you, mate.'

'James, it wasn't me - I swear it. It came from the woods. You heard it too!?'

'Well hell ye'a Oy hea'd it – it was clea as day! Someone was pliying a flute just outside of the ca'. I thought it was you – su'ely.'

'Someone's out there, James. It came from the woods, just at the tree-line, I could tell that much.'

'Well what did ya see?'

'Couldn't see anything – it's just black out there'

'Well hell, mate -- that's about the creepiest stuff that's eva happened to me. Whatd'ya reckon we get the heel out of hea?'

'Let's go,' I said with raised eyebrows and a crinkled forehead that he couldn't see.

CHAPTER 8

I was thinking about the plane ticket in my possession. Its departure was in five days from Dublin to Prague, Czech Republic. The day after our haunting, that's all James and I could talk about. If we finally thought the conversation was finished and a new topic had arisen, another one of us would break out saying something like 'My god, man – that was weird stuff. I still don't believe it. We must be losing our bloody minds.'

We were intent on finding something called The *Cliffs of Moher*, travelling dead north (my first time north again since the midge attacks). After another long day's drive, we stumbled on the cliffs at about 5:30 p.m. There were tourists everywhere at the entrance with a proper parking lot. It looked like they might be charging money, so we parked a half-mile down the road behind the remaining rubble of a stone house and cut through a cow pasture. From the car, it was nearly a mile walk up an open pasture to the cliff. We stumbled onto the abrupt edge at the top of the hill. Inches from my toes was a menacing drop to the death. I looked to my left and could see a five mile peninsula of cliff that jutted out into the crashing ocean below. It grew thin toward the end, and I could barely decipher a very small object at the end; it was a tower of some sort. I looked to my right and there were hundreds of people gathering on a properly built platform with safety walls and look-out binoculars thirty seconds to the dollar.

'How's left look to you?' I asked James.

'It's quite a ways out there. Could take the rest of the day, mate.'

'I'm down for it.'

'Alrighty.'

Some of the greenest hills I've ever seen rolled up and down during our walk to the end. We passed many adventurous walkers on their way back for the day. We were the only ones headed out. The gust coming off the ocean would knock a man to the ground if he wasn't paying close attention. I love it, though – the wind – the caressing hand of Mother Nature.

Hours later we arrived at a most glorious final destination. The stone building was collapsing. It was a medieval watch-tower.

When we looked back, we could not see the tourists because of sheer distance. We were now completely engulfed by the power of the Atlantic - amongst the three true super powers of earth: wind, water, and rock - who can humble any of us in seconds. I sat on my belly at the edge of the cliff at the farthest point of the peninsula, in a green and very comfortable type of grass, with my head facing west into the Ocean, toward my homeland. The gust pressed consistently against my face. It was so cold – even chilling to my ears and tearing to my eyes, but I still envy every second of it as I speak to you now. It was the most majestic place I'd ever seen on this planet, and it was all to myself – not a tourist in sight, except for James wandering around somewhere on the other side of the tower.

The sun was destined to set shortly and we had a considerable walk back. James beckoned for us to leave. I was reluctant to go. We walked back on the one and only trail, which many times became thin and forced a person towards the cliff's edge. Our tardiness to the *Cliffs of Moher* required us to walk back in the night. We did so with extreme calibration of each and every step. This added a great deal of time onto our walk and the stars were in full effect by the time we reached our car.

We decided to drive on and find a more appropriate spot to sleep. We feared the police might be near, considering the tourist area. We didn't want to be fined or jailed--who knows the laws somewhere else? We searched and searched for a place that would allow us a sure rest, which eventually brought us at a forest edge, once again. The walk provided our tired bodies with a peaceful sleep this time.

When morning came, the bright sun directed onto my face through the window had woken me. It wasn't the light that disturbed me, but rather, the warmth I felt on my thin eyelid. I left the car to do my morning business and walked up into the woods. It was the second most beautiful thing my eyes had ever seen to that point. A stream ascended slightly uphill and weaved through perfectly placed, extraordinarily tall pine trees. It was different because there was a peculiar moss that grew all throughout this forest. I had never seen moss grow on the typically dry underside of a pine, but clear as day, it grew there that day. It was such a bright green that it glowed like a lightning bug, and even seemed to generate more light so that I could see deep into the well-shaded forest.

The town where James and I were scheduled to depart wasn't far. I enjoyed his company after we became part-way comfortable with each other. I think he enjoyed mine also. Any company is better than being alone; it just took traveling alone to realize it. But with every turn of the corner, it seemed a new companion would await me, and I was already excited for the next.

We covered a ton of territory, driving at a grueling pace. The pace we moved at was tiresome. I knew I would be back to walking again soon and I actually looked forward to the slower pace it would bring. Left and right, left and right, up and down, we continued on the rugged Irish coastal roads toward our parting destination: Galway. I hardly paid any attention to the stunning coastal scenery anymore; but all things lose their special effect if we don't consume them in moderation. I was ready to move to the next destination.

With a cliff to our left, we began to enter a right-hand turn that was so sharp it forced our car to a turtles pace. Keep in mind, this is Ireland and were making this turn in the left lane. As we entered at the creeping pace, a car was passing equally slow. Barely attentive, I looked over and just happened to catch the driver of the other car, who by consequence, happened, also, to be staring at me directly in the eyes. He turned his head to maintain eye contact with me the whole way through the turn. His sharp features, powerful nose, and slick white hair were unmistakable. My heart stopped and I pressed myself tight in my seat. This time I couldn't help but to whisper my feelings out loud:

'Oh. My. God. *I swear* I saw that guy on the *other side of the country*!'

Immediately after the sharp turn, a gravel pull-off opened up and James slammed the breaks, skidding into it, and looked at me, saying:

'*Mate*! You have **got** to be kidding me! I thought the saime theeng too!'

He glared at me behind his dark glasses under his ball

cap, with an open mouth and I didn't know what to say. I was in shock, and not really sure if my mind was really playing tricks on me or not. It was the first time I ever felt that way in my life. James couldn't believe it, saying 'I saw that son of a beetch back in Deengle. You don't reckon he's follerin' us do ya?'

A man can do a lot of thinking while travelling by himself. I got to thinkin' a little about life and my conscience got all tangled up. My mama raised me right and so I act right. I was brought to the church most every Sundays for a long time when I lived at home. But nonetheless, I'd committed a considerable amount of sin right after I was turned loose, which is why I was sure; I am sure, that white haired beast was the reaper who followed me.

CHAPTER 9

As I exited the airplane into an open airfield, I noticed the immediate differences. The remnants of the Soviet Union were evident in several tanks and other war machines that stood alone in a rusting state of neglect. I knew America was on the other half of the weapons race, but I'd never seen proof of it abandoned at our international airports. I felt like a one man parade distributing smiles and hellos and handshakes that rarely received a returned gesture. I instantly adopted the necessary changes. Prague was cold, but I tried not to be too discouraged; I knew people in downtown New York City weren't acting extremely congenial either. I tried to keep in mind that these people were busy living real lives chasing the money, not some free-spirited fantasy like what I was doing.

So long as separate nations exist, they'll be driven by their underlying human instinct to compete for security and self-preservation; money, that is – thus continuing a perfectly natural cycle the existence of man has yet to break. I'm not blaming them; but we must realize it's not going to stop. The twentieth century was the bloodiest of all. We ought to embrace war as our nature and live content lives knowing it will never leave us – it is us. Every animal, insect, fish, and human is at war this very moment for their right to more property. Until the whites stop wanting to reproduce with whites, blacks to blacks, and Asian to Asian, it will continue - and that's simply not going to happen - we're simply robots for our DNA. They made us integrate back in school, but we segregated at lunch. It's difficult for white man, or any man, to relinquish his position of power in society because, ultimately, he fears that the human instinct of others is all too similar to his own: pack animals. The optimistic will ignore what I say. The futile will attempt to conceal what I say. And the ignorant - they will deny what I say, but it's truth that I bring to you, and any truth is always delicately maneuvered by the parties of the world.

Sorry about that, it just came out. Anyhow, I walked myself around Prague, Czech Republic after an entirely free plane ride. I went right to the downtown part of the city. First order of business was to try the food, so I got a huge Bohemian style hotdog that cost me a fortune. Next order of business - as usual - was trying the beer. The Czechs are known for their greatness in beer, and it does rival that of Germany and Latvia, but English Ale prevailed as my favorite. I was interested to find that their most well-known beer, *Budvar*, tasted like an improved American Budweiser. I was later informed that Budweiser somehow stole the recipe, which seemed undeniable based on the taste.

Walking in mid-afternoon down a crowded city square, I realized something odd. I almost missed it because it wasn't standing out, so-to-say, but as I listened, there was nearly complete silence for long moments at a time. All I heard were the sound of footsteps and the occasional flutter of pigeon wings. The people did not speak. There was no conversation, not any music or laughter, no smiles, no nothing. The expression of what I know to be human life dangled a rusty vacant sign and that was seriously strange for me.

Yet, I strolled around happily, embracing the best architecture in the world. Until, that is, the lovely sound of someone speaking English garnered my attention. It was good English, too, and for the next few months, I would find this a rarity. I approached this man and we became immediate friends. He was in his late twenties. He was there on business, but he was also looking for a good time, so we planned on a night out right away. Joris and I shared a room that night.

His hometown was Amsterdam, but he lived many years of his life in Germany. He was one of the finest friends I came to meet in all of Europe, and I later visited him at his parent's home in Karlsruhe, Germany and stayed for a while. As a frequent businessman to Prague, Joris warned me of the Gypsies. I never had any dealings with any Gypsies before. In fact, I didn't know anything about them at all.

We met another man named Asi in the lobby that evening before going out. He was a lone traveler, also on business. Asi physically matched the description of a Gypsy, and we were both wary of him. He was also in his late twenties. He wore a ponytail with jet black, thick, wavy hair. Asi told us he was from Israel and owned a private beach in Romania, running it as a vacation spot for party-goers. Anything and everything that came out of this guy's mouth sounded like it was a sale of some sort - everything ending with the words 'Trust me.'

That night, Asi looked at me many times in the eyes with a sincere look, saying 'Trust me. Trust your brother, Jesse' waving his finger a little. I never did trust him, but I still quite liked him. His English was also good, but not like Joris', who almost sounded like a surfer boy from Malibu. The two of them were on the same page as me with women. I've never walked next to a guy before where a huge portion of women that passed by would actually turn their heads for a second glance at him; girls in Prague, Germany, and France - all places we traveled together - did this to savor every possible moment with Joris. He wore a bandana to pull back his shoulder length brown hair. As a joke, Asi and I started calling him Jeff, because he just looked like a Jeff.

That night Asi took us to many places. He assured us he knew every inch of Prague and knew many people. Joris and I spoke once in private of our skepticism of him. 'Do we trust Asi?' he asked. 'I don't know. It seems he is lying to us about things, doesn't it?' But we continued with him anyway. There was safety in the relationship between the two of us. There was an immediate and certain connection of trust – no questions about it on either end.

Asi walked very fast wherever he went – even faster than James back in Cork. He smoked his cigarette mixed with marijuana right as he walked the city streets. He claimed no one cared, not even police. I wasn't sure about that one. He said to me and Joris in his Middle Eastern accent: 'Come, come. Follow me,' gesturing with his hand. 'Trust your brother – come.' he would provoke again as we walked. 'I will take you to a place where are my good friends.' We rung a doorbell and went down into a basement filled with smoke. Heavy Metal was blasting in another room. Everyone looked at us as we walked through. It was a private bar and also a tattoo parlor.

'These are my great friends, I promise you,' he said when Jeff and I asked for reassurance. We didn't seem to be welcome by the look on anyone's face. I asked for a beer and the bartender looked the other way. 'Do not worry, that is just how they are in Czech, I promise you. We are welcome here, trust me.' It was a rough place. The guys were pretty tough looking fellows with all their tattoos. Everyone was tattooed, in fact, and dressed in black. Asi said 'Look, here is my good friend coming now,' speaking of the bar tender that turned harshly rejected me. Asi turned his back to us, leaned inward to the bar and spoke softly so we could not to hear him. The man got him beers and maybe even spoke a word back, but I couldn't be sure they were friends. He may have even seemed like he didn't know Asi at all, but I couldn't be certain of that either. Joris and I looked at each other and sort of smiled while raising an eyebrow. We drank our round of beers and talked. After that, Joris suggested we go somewhere else, so we did.

We went to a few other bars where I felt a bit more comfortable, but never extremely welcome. Asi said he knew of a place that would blow our minds, and he would takes us later in the night. After the fourth or fifth bar, it was well past midnight, I'd say. Joris decided he wanted to go home, and I was left with the decision to go with Asi into the early hours of the morning to somewhere on the outskirts of the city: One: far away from my belongings, which were loosely secured at the hole we were staying in, and Two: with the likes of Asi.

I trusted my brother and went with Asi. We walked fast, and turned many corners. I struggled to maintain the route home, until I was forced to only focus on maintaining a general direction of where I was – that is, in relation to everything I had gathered in a casual day's walk of the city. He took me on and off several bus routes, and considering the ten beers at the previous bars, I was entirely lost now – only speculation of a general direction was left. While riding a bus I grew anxious, and inquired if we were close. The fast paced, speed-talking salesman took care of my silly questions in no time. He was born this way, then raised this way – couldn't help it. But when I didn't let him win and asked more specific question so there *could be no* bullshit, he stopped and looked at me. This, he had not done before, and said sincerely, 'Jesse, I am your brother - you must trust me now - - until I have done you some distrust.' I liked this. I admire another man that can be so sincere. We walked six or seven confusing blocks after the second bus route, somewhere outside of Prague - I think on the south side, but not positive.

We came to a door that looked like absolutely nothing. The biggest man I'd ever seen stood just inside, who Asi had several quiet words with. Asi spoke a little Czech, but also four other languages fluently: Hebrew, English, Arab, and Romanian. We walked through a tight passageway and down a stairwell made of stone. At the end stood a man double my size, but not as big as the first. He pointed with his fingers to our right (one of the three possible directions) and we walked down a stairwell in another tight passage between stone walls. At the end was another man almost as large, and there were three more passageways to go through. I heard music; otherwise I would have started fighting my way back to the exit for dear life, but still, I was unbelievably skeptical. I'd heard crazy stories of these people kidnapping people to sell their organs, and you can be certain I thought of this. The man directed us into the right passageway, toward the music. We looked at the stone archway where he pointed, then proceeded through it. I felt my way along a cold stone wall to the light at the end of the tunnel.

We entered a room that was long and highly rectangular. The walls were lined with booths and a wide isle in between, with a red carpet. Four sets of steep, spiraling iron stairs allowed access to private balconies at the perimeter of the ceiling. There were people dangling their feet between the railings of all four balconies, overlooking the room. Asi and I sat at a booth. A young woman brought us two beers and I don't ever recall being stopped in my tracks like I was here by such pure and mysterious beauty.

I got a chance to copy down the faces of people dangling from the balcony around me. There were many young girls who were all smoking and drinking beers. I noticed they were watching me. Each booth was entirely private and separated from the others. They were large and extremely luxurious and comfortable. The seat went up to the back of my neck, and from there, all the way to the tall ceiling were bars of unique and artistic ironwork. They were hand crafted – artwork like I had never seen. I looked up at the lighting of our private booth, which was very close to my head, and the chandelier was moving. The lights were hidden within an intricate system of steel gears and all sorts of polished metal parts - all of which were in *constant motion*. This system hung from the ceiling on several camshafts from cars, which were also in motion as its function would be in a moving car. I looked around the club and everything was like this; a piece of art – the whole place. Asi saw me looking around in complete fascination and said 'Eh? Didn't I tell you, Jesse? – The craziest shit you have ever seen, no? What did I tell you? I want you to tell me – what did I tell you, my friend?' I looked toward him over the table and couldn't help but to smile, saying 'Trust your brother, I know.' I laughed with relief once and we laughed together once more. It *was* truly an amazing place like I had never experienced before or after – and that was just the first room.

'Now. Let us live. You see the women? Eh? No? Magnificent!'

'Some of these girls are like twelve or thirteen years old,' I rebuked.

'Who cares about the age. You are in Prague, my friend. You do what you want in Prague. Do you not see me? I smoke in the streets, no one cares. And there is no age here for those girls, I will tell you this. We will talk to some of them, now - watch.'
He motioned for one group of girls in the balconies to come to us. Three girls came and sat down. They were thirteen and fourteen; Czech girls. I don't think they were prostitutes, but the street corners at night were lined with thirteen year old Russian girls, helpless and void of any possible rescue. Those girls looked beaten, drugged, and worn – all of them, and seeing them made me feel more sad than I ever have in my life. It helped me appreciate the United States and my patriotism for it. But these girls weren't prostitutes, like I said. They tried to talk with us in English, and didn't do too badly. I figured they were just learning English from school. After short conversation, they stood up to go dance and invited us to come.

I pardoned myself from the booth for a bathroom break, which was down another passageway. When I returned, the girls were gone. Asi said 'Come on, Jesse, lets go dance with the girls. It is no problem here, you must trust me. You are not in America where it is so uptight; no one here cares. The girls do not care - they want you. Don't you see?'

'You don't understand. I just can't do that. I haven't been

taught like that, Asi. They're just little girls – look at them.'

'They may be little girls to you, but women to me, women to all men here, and women to the government.'

'Well I'm sorry'

'Your country has damaged your mind. My brother…We have two possibilities in this life: to follow the instinct or to follow the rules,' he said.

'Those rules are called ethics and morals, brother, and when the world loses them, it goes back to the dark ages again.'

'What?! The dark ages, do you speak of. There never are dark ages in this world – it has all been the same forever; people have not changed. The Jews crumbled the Roman Empire with a simple story and so now you think this because all real knowledge is hidden from you. You think the Christian sheet or the Muslim sheet has made some difference? Bullsheet! The only thing that matters is the parents. You ask of the Gypsies – I know these Gypsies all my life. But I am not like them. You know why? My father -your father - tell us "Jesse. You do not to steal" – and you do not steal. My father says to me, Asi! You do not steal, never! And now, I do not steal – never. But your father tells you to believe in some God, and you do this also, so the reason why we have more war than ever before. Let me tell you thees: I am from Israel - I have seen some sheet. This is nothing.

'Well, maybe I haven't seen too much shit in America, but I'm happy about it. And there aren't little girls being sold on the streets there. I know that much. And until recently, it *has* been a Christian world. The object is to resist instinct. Don't you think? Jealousy, sex, hate, war – all instincts.

'What!; you will just lock us all behind the bars? We are just the animal too; you will put us in a zoo? I do not like thees idea of zoo. Have you ever been to a zoo? It is spooky, no? - Some terrible feelings come when you go inside - all things locked up in cages; human must be free too. Sheet, this conversation is too difficult for my English, come with me now – I will show you something.'

We finished our beers quickly and walked toward a passageway at the other end of the booth room. Another big Czech guy stood there. Asi spoke to him, then we passed. I spent a lot of time studying the stone work throughout Europe, and as a result, I became able to date much of the stuff by looking at the building techniques and the design. I wasn't always exactly right, but I could get very close most of the time. I tested it often. I speculated this club was built inside a six hundred year old cellar/dungeon of some sort. It was massive. The passageways kept going and going. We went deeper and deeper, down more stairwells, until I lost my direction inside the place entirely. It seemed like it was a maze, designed to confuse.

We came to another larger room and walked through. The only light came from the room we were walking toward, but I could still see the faces of people leaning and sitting against the walls. Many stared at me as I walked by, several taking their attention off conversations. We heard very loud music ahead. There was flashing white light with lots of fog coming from the end and to the right side of the hypothetical room that was there. We breeched the end of the dark room, and around the corner was another, even larger room with a band playing on stage. There were about one hundred people dancing, watching, smoking, drinking, and kissing. The music was a hard techno made through instruments. It was an extravagant show. The band looked like they were from the Twenty Fifth Century yet to come; their dress, their instruments, their makeup. The floor beneath my feet was glass, and below the glass were old television sets that were turned on. Some showed scrambled things, some were set on flat colors such as blue or red, and others were playing various videos. While I was examining the floor, I noticed something crawling on the ground between people's feet. It crawled toward me and then stopped. It was a tiny teenage Asian girl. She wore a shiny, silver, one piece bathing suit - to very poorly describe it. Her makeup, hair and dress, also, were like something I'd never seen before: from the future. But she wore something across her eyes also: a silver plastic piece, with a black strip going across the middle -- tinted-like material which allowed her to see out of; much like something from star-trek. In her hand was a Chinese fan. After she stopped right at my feet, she looked up at me, tilted her head sideways like a robot and waved that fan at my face with her arm out straight, accompanied by a huge smile. She then hobbled off on all four limbs. I looked at Asi in amazement. He and I walked closer to the stage where the band played and I saw more tiny Asian girls hobbling around.

Pretty soon, Asi and I had more beers and he got to talking to more thirteen year old girls. I turned around once, and he was gone - no where to be found. I didn't worry too much; I stayed a while and listened to music and tried to talk to some people. When I attempted to exit the club, I went to several of the doorways where the big guys stood in black. They wouldn't let me pass. The first said 'No. Go!' and I remained a moment, then tried to proceed through anyway. He grabbed my arm really tight, then pushed me and yelled something really angry in his language. I wasn't frantic, but getting close to it. I walked to another exit and right away the guy at the door said to me in a despicable voice: 'You fucking American!' He knew I was American - I don't know how, but he did. That exit-way was blocked, so I went to the last one that was left, where there was a small lobby that had three other connecting exits. I stood in the intersection thinking for a second, then another guy in black yelled English curses at me and said 'OUT!' as if he were very upset and if I didn't leave, I was sure to be murdered down here without question. I moved fast to the left when he said this to avoid trouble, which brought me to a small room I hadn't yet seen. Five or ten people sat on the couches that lined the perimiter. At the other end of this room was a guy in black beside the entrance to another, yet again, dark passageway. As I proceeded to walk through, he stepped in front of me and bumped my shoulder hard, pushing me into the wall and I stopped and stared at him. It was time I stepped my game up and stopped getting bossed around. Something really bad was going on. They all knew I was American. I now understood that I was not welcome in this club, and they were all aware of my presence. My escort had disappeared. This guy wasn't bigger than me, but at this point I didn't care how big any of them were. I was losing my temper. We stared each other in the eyes momentarily, and I made the good decision to put my head down and walk through the passage. He didn't say anything.

At the end, there was another intersection with stairs going up to the right and down to the left. I went up to the right. I came to the top of those steps and there stood a guy in black, again, with his chest facing me as to say I couldn't pass. I kept my head down and stepped into the gap beside him, brushing his clothing against my own. He allowed it. I thought I was familiar with where I was now. Straight in front of me was the original set of stairs that I had come down, through the dark, narrow stairwell. When I got to the top of the steps, it flattened out to about fifteen feet of dark passageway with the exit door propped open. In front of it was the biggest guy of all from the entrance. He completely covered the exit. My adrenaline still rushed from all the previous encounters. My heart pumped through my chest as I thought frantically of what to do. I glanced up at him and he was staring straight at me. I put my head back down very casually. My instinctual senses evaluated his intentions in a split second and it indicated he didn't plan to let me pass. That instinct then sparked the development of a split second strategy to my dilemma. I walked peacefully toward him with my head toward the ground to exhibit passiveness. I didn't even think at this point – other forces commandeered my actions. When I got nearer to him – around five feet or so – I made my move. With all of my might and speed, I charged at him. With my hands out, I got low and used my legs and drove into him with everything I had. More was on the line for me than for him. He was powerful, and resisted me immediately. He tried to grab onto the walls, but I kept pushing and his hands slid from their brief grip. He almost had me stopped with that, but when his left foot stepped out of the doorway, it gave him a lower center of gravity, and I thought I was finished. This man would crush me. But it actually put him back just enough to allow me to sneak a foot into the crevice of the doorway and push with all my might. I drove hard from the legs and core of my body, delivering one more monster push. He tried to hang onto my wrist, but I broke the grip and took off running faster than ever onto the shiny wet streets of Prague.

CHAPTER 10

Several many weeks later, I found myself in the safety of the countryside once again. English was only something I thought to myself. I had just woken up in an abandoned barn. I stretched a bit, said hello to the sun, and started out on my way. It was a tepid sunny August afternoon. There was a slight crosswind that carried clouds like white elephants stampeding across the road as I walked the straight, flat stretch. I felt like I was in Kansas, or Missouri maybe, although I've been to neither. There were very few people around except farmers. There was no limit on the capability of the eye. I was somewhere in Poland near the border of Ukraine, heading north.

There wasn't any particular stupefying scenery here, but I still enjoyed the day - reveling, embracing and exercising the complete and utter freedom at hand. It was freedom that could electrify even the most dismal soul. I didn't have much luck with rides, because there just plum weren't any cars. The rides that I did accept were only going a few miles up the road, but I took anything that stopped; how could I tell how far they were headed with the language barrier? They could have been headed a mile up the road or all the way to Moscow.

When you're sleeping in foreign barns across the world, hitchhiking, flat broke but free, whether you got piss drunk the night before, or you're just a total couch potato every other day of the week, I don't know why this is, but you don't waste the daylight. It's evident that life is a constant race against the sun's righteous path through the sky. So I woke up very early and began, yes, you guessed it -- walking. It must have been four or five hours, because the sun, I remember, was nearing its highest point in the sky. I often turned around and walked backwards, walked in the middle of the road on the yellow lines, whatever I wanted − there weren't any cars coming. I owned the road as far as I knew or cared. The horizon became a good friend of mine and I watched him often. Remember, this wasn't the first day he and I became acquainted. About the same time as I exercised my ownership of the yellow line in the road, something crossed my line of sight just above the horizon behind me. It was nearly in the farthest distance

I could see. I couldn't decipher what it was exactly, so I kept on moving. But it never left. I kept looking back as I continued to walk. It remained visible for many miles. Thousands of grueling steps went by as my curiosity continued to grow. Finally, I'd had enough. Where was I going that I didn't have time to indulge in my curiosity? It's one of the greatest joys we have, so I decided to take a break and wait a while.

I let it come within a mile or two, where I could finally see space between what looked to be… people. I could not determine how many just yet, but they seemed to cover the width of the entire road. I let them advance even closer; a half mile possibly. But I chickened out and started to walk again as to further could study the situation. Safety is number one! It could easily have been an angry lynch mob with torches, out for their Cold War revenge.

I walked another ten minutes to keep them safely behind, but I soon got to thinking about who they were and what they were doing out here, so I stopped and let them approach. Needless to say, it seemed like eternity. I paced back and forth evaluating potential situations. Their advance was steady. Now I could see not only people, but also a large object hoisted over their heads. The closer they came, the more time slowed and my patience grew thin. A quarter mile out, I could distinguish the object: the wooden stake I was to be burned on. It was enormous -- forty feet long, at least. They must have heard how big Americans are.

Within a football field's length, things were revealed. Fifteen people were spread out on all ends of a large cross, some struggling more than others to keep it overhead. Other people made a circle around the cross, and if I wasn't mistaken, they seemed to be dancing. It looked like girls; all girls. I awaited their precession sitting on the ground. Our faces became increasingly defined to the sight. All of them were looking right at me, and I was playing it cool, still on the ground. They came within feet of me and we hadn't exchanged a word. They uniformly laid the tree-sized cross to the road. It didn't appear just yet that they wanted to harm me. I got up from the ground to greet them and there I stood staring at everyone – they, right back at me, resembling the first meeting between two intelligent life forms. Then, one of the girls spoke. It was a different language, and I just smiled at her like a dummy, still in disbelief of the situation. The girls were all beautiful, and I thought it a lovely little circumstance. Another girl made an attempt to speak to me and I didn't understand her either - I just turned my palms upward at my waist asking "what?"

Then the funniest thing happened: a man stepped forward from the crowd and said 'Hi, I'm Mike,' and put his hand out for a shake. I put my head back and started laughing a little. That caused an outbreak of confused gossip in the feminine crowd behind him until I said 'Pleased to meet you Mike. The name's Jesse,' in a confident, assured, and welcoming manner. He laughed also, knowing right away what I was.

'Should I even ask what in the world you're doing out here?' Mike started.

'Oh, you know: just enjoying an afternoon walk. Ya'll workin' for a timber company?' I asked sarcastically looking at the cross on the ground.

'Not quite. I'm a preacher from Ohio leading this group.'

'Leading them to what?'

'On a walk of faith.'

'Where to?'

'One of the towns up that-a way' he glanced with his eyes in the only direction one would suspect. 'We're taking this cross as our test. Would you like to join us?'

'Looks like it's destined to be.'

So they lifted the cross over their shoulders and we got on walking. Mike was at the head of the cross and I walked beside him. Our time together lasted three hours, so I figure we went about ten miles together. The beautiful girls wasted no time in resuming their dance around the cross. They also joined together in song. Their voices were certainly beautiful, but it was in a different language and I never much cared for hearing song out of a different tongue. I knew they were celebrating Christianity, but for a brief moment, as they danced around me, I could only think of witchcraft. It didn't take much imagination to make them witches as they pranced in circles chanting things. Instead of Joy to the World, which it probably was, I somehow found myself imagining it was a satanic summoning, which, thinking back now, is kind of reasonable.

Mike started out our conversation as a very typical guy. He was nice and we talked about normal subjects like baseball and Ohio State football. But I knew he'd drop the big bomb on me eventually, and, of course, he eventually did. It came with an abrupt and serious change of tone:

'You know I need to talk with you about something, Jess.

'Oh? What's that?' I knew before he introduced himself.

'Whether you have faith in the good lord Jesus Christ'

And for a long time I did, I could say for certain. But within the last years of my life, that certainty dwindled to a maybe. I was raised by a Christian family, and as far as anyone in the world knew, I was a Christian. At the point of this very question I had not even been able to consciously reject baby Jesus in my own mind, let alone with words that actually exited my mouth. When I was introduced to the idea of free-will over predestination I took off with it and haven't stopped the free-thinking since. Blame it on that.

I had two choices here: I could take the easy way or the hard way. But I wasn't going to lie to a man carrying a cross, so I said:

'I've never told anyone this before, but I've lost my faith Mike.'

God why did I say that?! I thought to myself right away.

'That's a serious problem, Jesse. Why do you think that happened?'

'You aren't going to like this, but I have a difficult time coping with the possibility that I'm being tricked.'

'What do you mean... tricked?'

'Well, you know; the Greeks had Zeus, and the Romans had Jupiter and those guys -- and now we snicker at *them* for believing such foolish things. I don't want to be the fool in another 2,000 years. You know what I mean?'

'No. I don't. Nor do I understand how *the Romans* could possibly have an effect on your faith. Those gods weren't real.'

Which confused me. I thought it was pretty clear: it's history, which is knowledge and therefore, reason. How can I be asked by god to give up the one and only that is, with a certainty, my own?

'I don't know, Mike, I just think bad things sometimes. I don't know why I do it.' I admitted.

'Like what?'

'I guess I'm paranoid.'

'I'm not following you.' He seemed frustrated already.

'Okay; you really want to know? For starters, I think that Santa Clause was fabricated to train children to think in terms of faith. You know, what you practice as a child, you practice as an adult -- usually. Like when your father tells you, 'Mike, you do not steal," and so you do not steal when you're a man – never. If you learned to have faith in Santa Clause as a boy, you're trained to have faith in God. See?'

'No. I don't see. I fear for you, son. I don't know where you are getting these ideas from, but they're bad, I see that. The devil is working within you, and you must believe it. He works in the corner of our minds sometimes, and the only way to release yourself from his hold is to find the light – the light of Jesus, our savior. Those other religions were pagan - ritualistic - they killed animals, raped girls and boys – they were fabrications. Jesus is living proof. Look around you. He's here with us right now. Can't you feel him in our presence?' He asked with one eyebrow lifted high and his head tilted slightly down.

I was being deadly honest here so that Mike might truly offer me some guidance. I was keeping an open mind to possibly even challenge the previous open mind that had gotten me here. It wasn't working. It didn't help that he seemed to be getting angry the more I spoke my mind. I created my ideas myself. I didn't read them or go searching for some sacrilegious dribble on purpose. They were just a result of pure reason. His irritability only worsened as we continued:

'How could one man transform the world in such a short time – the world that killed him, nonetheless?'

'True.'

'Look at the bible alone, Jesse. Have you read it?'

'Some.'

'It is a divine act in itself – a miracle of writing; much too complicated for anyone to up and create.'

'It does seem unlikely, you are right,' I argued against myself. But I changed that quickly and said 'Well, that book *was* formed at the Council of Nicea in the fourth century after Rome gathered 300 of its top thinkers to settle the matters of Jesus.'

He was unfamiliar with what I said and changed the subject. The girls were still dancing and singing around us.

'You need to ask yourself, what should we live life for?'

'I think…for freedom'

'But that's selfish and instinctual – the very problem with this world. You should live for Christ – he died for you and lived for you.'

'And he *could be* regretting that decision based on what's happened since he's left.'

Yet another argument of reason left unattended.

'You need to decide something now, Jesse, and never go back. You cannot continue to live for yourself - for those selfish, selfish reasons. Neither can you carry-on and indulge and continue to sin without repent. You'll end up somewhere you don't want to be, trust me. What you need to do - here and now - is accept Christ, Jesse, and join me in spreading the good word. Help change this world for the better. Leave that self-involved world you live in. Leave your mark by doing God's will. He has a plan in mind for you. I can see it now, and it's a great one.'

'My mark? I don't even want to be remembered. I think being buried – having a tombstone with your name – *that's* selfish – for taking up all that space; it's something that was created by someone who was terrified of being forgotten. Burn me, *please*; put me right into the stars where I belong - I'm anxious to join them. If a man truly wants to leave behind a legacy, all he needs to do is perform good deeds. Its effects will butterfly into eternity. That's the mark I'll leave.'

The look on his face worried me for myself.

'Jesse, would you mind if we prey for you?'

I still figured in the possibility I did need preyed for, so I accepted. He put the cross down in the middle of the road and everyone stopped. They all surrounded me holding hands. Mike asked if I would please go to my knees. I did. He then grabbed the front and back of my head tightly and the girls started to chant. This wasn't any style of prayer I was used to, but I closed my eyes while Mike said it anyhow:

'Oh gracious father, I call on you in a time of need. In the midst of my journey I have encountered a son of yours who has lost his way. He is blind, and I beg of you oh father, help him see. He has fallen and he *needs* you to stand back up. He lives a life surrounded by darkness and we beg of you, oh father, *please* bring him to the light. His heart has become tainted with evil, and sin. Satan lurks in the corners of his imagination and leads him to temptation.' And his voice began to rise here, 'I ask of you now, lord: open him up and put the holy spirit in him! Let that spirit flourish to ward off the devil - the sickness that he is! Please lord, help Jesse destroy *all* those terrible faculties of instinct and reason that infiltrate his *soul*! - making faithful service to god *the only* reason for our brother Jesse.

Oh, I feel it now - the lord is here. He *is* upon us! You have this one chance – this one and last chance, my son. It's a beautiful gift coming straight toward you. Accept Jesus Christ and never go back! Walk a righteous life beside him, full of beautiful faith, just as we walk here now. In the name of the lord! *Receive* him now!' and he pushed my head so hard that I had to use my hands to brace my fall.'

I heard the girls stop singing. When I looked up, they were all staring at me like they expected something. We stood up and resumed our walk like nothing had happened. No one was singing - just walking. Silence. I no longer walked at the head of the pack with Mike, just to the outside somewhere. We walked like this for a few moments before one girl approached me from the other side of the cross and asked sweetly in broken English:

'Did you accept Jesus Christ?'

CHAPTER 11

I wandered about much of Eastern Europe, enjoying a relief from the high prices of the west. But I grew terribly lonesome and worn. After illegally crossing the Russian border, I moved through Estonia, then Latvia when the fever hit. One bright afternoon I found myself face down in the dirt on the side of a busy roadway only miles outside the city of Riga. The world behind me was spinning like a bad dream. A man named Sydney stopped and picked me up and I slept on his couch for three days until the fever broke. I'd never been so grateful as this. But there's no sense in telling you about all the normal people, when there's so many strange ones left.

When I left Sydney, I was coming down through Lithuania, about to make a right turn and head west. I had many uneventful rides out there, but not this one; I'll never forget it. It was another beautiful day with a blue sky and more white fluffy clouds floating across the flat, straight stretch of road in front of me. It looked no different than the last place I told you about. The cars and population were just as scarce.

A junky car pulled to the shoulder. Mind you, we're now driving on the right side of the road. As I approached, I was a bit nervous about who may be inside, as always. The car's broken muffler hummed extra loud when I walked by it. The window was down and I crouched to look inside. It was an old woman waving me on and smiling. I was pleased and jumped right in. She accelerated immediately, and I was relieved to be inside any type of shelter and to sit in a padded seat. I remember my feet hurting badly and I was still only recuperating. This was a good opportunity to sleep, I thought. The woman looked like she was pushing eighty years old. Her hair was dyed red and pulled nicely up into a bun. There was a distinct grey streak running up the side of her head visible to me. She seemed sweet and really old, so I closed my eyes and rested on and off. I wasn't paying attention to anything, really. I hardly cared what direction we went or where she took me; I knew it was south – that was fine. I was too tired to be concerned. Her head seemed to bobble left and right as she drove, but I didn't pay any mind to that either.

We stopped for gas after an hour of driving and I woke up to use the restroom. I didn't figure an old bird like her knew any English, but when we resumed driving she ended the silence between us. She looked over at me and struggled very slowly to say three words:

'God... bless... you.'

'Thank you,' I smiled.

'You...are... American?'

'Yes, I am.'

'My daughter... in America ... with man'

'Oh, great. Do get to see her?' I asked pointing to my eyes.

'No, I do... not.'

'I'll bet you miss her.'

'Miss? Ahhh, miss' she smiled for remembering the word

'Yes, I miss. . . very much her. She teach... some English with me.'

Our conversation was limited, so we weren't able to continue much longer. I wanted to go back to Poland in order to head west again, and I conveyed this to her. She seemed to understand and indicated she would take me to the exact road I needed. I wish I could remember her name, but I can not. All I have now is a picture of her two frail hands holding onto the steering wheel at nine o'clock and three o'clock. She had her seat adjusted so her chest was right against the steering wheel. I also noticed earlier that she was not steady with her hands. She was shaking so much that the steering wheel constantly moved left and right. It made our car swerve to the left and right of our lane, but there were no cars on the country road and she was going slow, so I wasn't too badly concerned.

At some points she seemed "With it," and others, not so much. I learned more about her as the drive went on by my observation. Her shaking worsened the longer we drove. There were several instances in which she laughed for no apparent reason. And it wasn't any normal laugh, but a wretched shrieking laugh. The first time she did it, she looked over at me while she was doing it and I noticed her brown, rotted teeth. She had other strange behaviors, like a tick in her face that made her look angry all of a sudden. It actually frightened me. She had sporadic behaviors that I can't explain. It all got worse.

We had driven up a ramp that put us onto a larger road. It was still only two lanes, but it was better pavement and there was a great deal more traffic. Many big tractor-trailers traveled there. The speed limit was also increased. As soon as we were dumped onto this road, the old woman hit the gas all the way to the floor, which dropped the car down a gear and put me tight in my seat. The car's capabilities surprised me. She surprised me. We continued increasing speed and were approaching one of the big trucks quickly. I held tight to the door, turning my knuckles white. She straddled the yellow lines and right before we hit the truck, she swerved hard left and we were passing him in the opposite lane. I was relieved to see a clear path in front of us. We got back into our lane and continued at high speeds. It must have been eighty miles per hour. The next big truck was in sight and I was bracing even tighter. She wasn't able to keep the car steady at all. We swerved left and right even more radically. I looked at her and said something frantically in English which she ignored - maybe it was 'What are you doing!?' Again she hugged the yellow line strategizing her next pass. She went to make her move around this truck, but a car was coming and she made a hard right back into our lane right as the opposing car whipped passed us only feet away. My adrenaline was going hard. Before I could say anything, she hit the gas once more, going into the opposite lane. A car was coming at us in the distance and I yelled 'Stop, stop, stop!' She kept going. It seemed like the big truck to my right would never pass by. We reached the gap between the cargo and the truck and I could see we weren't going to make it. I again yelled 'Stop, stop!' bracing tight for impact. I was prepared to grab the wheel from her, but she forced the other car onto the shoulder of the road before we hit. He slammed on his breaks and we squeezed by, and went back into our lane. She was laughing her deranged laugh and looked over at me at me with her brown teeth. I yelled at her 'You're crazy!' I was sweating all over. This was mad. Our speed was still above eighty and we seemed constantly on the verge of wrecking. 'Please,' I said 'please.' She was not concerned with my begging – the more I spoke the faster she went. 'God bless you' she replied with her eyes focused on the road. The break in traffic didn't last long. Time went quickly. We approached a line of three or four cars. She hugged the middle of the road, prepared to pass.

'No, slow down! Slow down!' I pleaded

So she veered into the opposing lane and laughed the entire time. Another car was coming for us and we definitely weren't going to make it. She intended to run them off the road. And again, she did. I was screaming 'ahhhhhh' the whole time it was happening this time. The car was forced to the edge and death passed by me only feet away. She seemed to take pleasure from it.

'God bless you' she told me many times over, 'God bless you.'

I went through one or two more near-death experiences before she impulsively decided to drive normally behind traffic. I thought many times take to control of the wheel, but never got the courage. I was convinced this lady was possessed by something. She forced me to say my prayers. I was speechless after this happened. It all went so quickly and I didn't react. We drove another half an hour together and she stopped the car and pointed ahead, saying 'Poland.' She intended to take another road. I got out of the car and started walking. I wasn't angry. I wasn't upset or sad. I was in a crazed state of mind. I didn't say goodbye, I just walked. I didn't get far before I heard her reverse the car beside me. The window was down and I didn't even bother to look inside at her. I just heard her say 'God bless you, son.'

CHAPTER 12

I made it through northern Poland and crossed the border into Germany. I explored many of their cities and tasted all of their beers. I hadn't had a good meal for a while. Every morning I woke up, I would find the nearest grocery store and purchase a loaf of bread, cheese, and some tomatoes, as always. This lasted me the whole day usually. I refilled a plastic water bottle in public sinks.

I remember arriving to Berlin late on a Thursday night. I was somewhere in the center city business district. I was exhausted and looking for a safe place to sleep. My body was beaten down from hundreds of miles of walking, it was dirty, and not very well nourished. I watched many groups of young German men and women the same age as me heading out for the night. They walked right by me without noticing. They were excited and laughing together. I thought of my life like this at home. I watched them revel in their comfortable lives, while I was painfully delighted to be liberated from those same comforts. After I sat a while, watching the German youth, I walked down an alleyway looking for a place to sleep, but this alley was already occupied. It was dark, but I could see their faces looking at me with the streetlights at my rear. Several men were laying on their backs against the walls of the buildings to my left and right. The one to my right had his shoes off and I could see his dirty toes sticking up in the air. I stopped for a moment to think of what I should do. After evaluating the situation, I decided they may be dangerous and I walked back out to the open city street. I fell asleep that night under the doorway of a huge corporate skyscraper where I would certainly be safe. In the morning I woke to the sound of high heels and the soles of men's shoes walking by my head. The sun was warm and disturbed me worse than the clicking of shoes. I was now just one of the men from the alley.

My travels were similar to this through many other German cities. I found the German's to be the friendliest people in all of Europe, and even in their cities people invited me to stay in their homes. I made my way to the south where I arrived at the doorstep of my friend Joris, from the Czech Republic. He insisted I sleep in his bed and so he slept on his couch for nearly a week. While

I stayed there I was able to completely rejuvenate my body. My spirit was stronger than ever, though, and needed no rest; freedom cures all. My soul, however, came into question in the coming travels.

I explored the south of Germany and roamed around the black forest. I was near the border of France, so all the while, my French heritage called on me. I was antsy to find it. I knew that my ancestors had come from the Alsace-Lorraine territory between France and Germany. It's not easy being an American. Europeans don't understand. You love your country and your land, but may have only lived there, say, twenty years; meanwhile, a land exists out there that your ancestors - the blood inside you - have formed a union with for potentially thousands of years.

Finally I crossed into the border of France; a place, I found, of an exceedingly proud people. I often wondered by what faculties they came to reside at this disposition. As I travelled farther into Alsace-Lorraine, I realized why, for one example, my attempts to order food in English were harshly declined by one mechanism or another: it was arguably the most beautiful land my eyes had ever seen. Admittedly, this opinion may have been bias by my genetic predisposition to the region. But my travel across Alsace truly allowed me to understand how the French could have come to their current demeanor. It's difficult for an American to understand, I think, for total lack of a similar experience, but the French have been under a perpetual challenge to maintain not only the Alsace region, but all of France, their culture and language from the surrounding English, German and Spanish; a task to be respected. The history of this impressive land, unfortunately, as a result of the human capacity to pursue his desires of general acquisition, is not surprisingly marked by that of siege. An overwhelming amount of French history is marked by such. So we must also contract that French have a history of not only fighting to defend property, but also the aforementioned: language and culture, which at the time of later gobbling the hell out of my McDonald's cheeseburger, after a most valiant fight with hand gestures and scrambled English, did I completely realize this in one abrupt moment of time, staring out a window.

I knew my ancestors were farmers around a town called Metz. I asked around and headed straight for it. I stopped in many small places along the way. I negotiated with the people for rides and found it quite difficult. After my interactions with the French accumulated in my travel from Strausburg, where I entered France, to the town of Metz, I became confused; these didn't seem to be my people at all. They were very small with darker features. I felt like a giant amongst the French. When I made it to Metz I stopped for a beer in a pub. I methodically sipped on it because I couldn't buy another that day. I was pleased to speak with the bartender who spoke English quite well. I think he said he was Puerto Rican and French. He was very informative on the area, and when I inquired about my ancestral dilemma, I think he resolved my problem. He told me that since the Alsace-Lorraine area had been warred over between the German and French, there were a considerable amount of Germanic people in the area who later became French. I think I had finally found the lost connection I was searching for.

That evening I left Metz feeling more satisfied than ever. Like all French towns in the area, the community limits end abruptly, opening to vast farmland. I walked out of town several miles and settled in for an early night's sleep. I was headed to Paris in the morning. I found a nice barn that was far secluded from a farmer's house. I didn't ask permission. As the sun set and night slowly seeped in, I was at peace. It was a calm and cool night. I fell asleep when the last hint of day passed away.

I carried a journal with me during this travel. I wrote in it every few days. I don't know how to say this. I haven't told anyone this before. All that my memory permits me to access is a vague picture of me writing in my journal that night with a small flashlight I have. I was conscious, but not. It's like I was in a delirium. I remember it only like a dream. I thought it was a dream at the time, but when I woke in the morning, I saw that it was no dream. I had written spastically over many pages. I wrote things that scared me – things that I didn't previously know – and in a manner I would never write. I even wrote in a different language at times: Old English, which I had studied before, but could only read at thirty percent understanding at best, and could not write. The things I wrote were biblical, but not in the bible. I only feel obliged to tell you that the writings ended with the repetition of the words 'tell them' and 'write it.' This story is not what the pages asked me to tell.

CHAPTER 13

The series of events behind me were strange. I can hardly believe it myself, but you must – it only continues. Everything in this book is truth, and I've got a perfectly good head on my shoulders. My walk to Paris was a tough one and took much longer than expected, but the worst was yet ahead. The French didn't seem to want to give me rides. As I walked all those miles, all I did was think and explore the depths of my mind. I got my conscience all tangled up over this stuff and couldn't seem to stop.

I felt comfortable with my probable body odor for once. Why not, I thought - I was in France – frolicking with my ancestry. I tried hard to forget about God. The new thoughts I acquired were only something I wanted to block out. But my encounters simply would not allow it to be vanquished.

I was out late that night on the streets of Paris. I sat in outdoor café's hoping to meet a friend to talk with, but no one took an interest in me. Paris continued-on that night without even flinching that I was there. I went to some streets where a lot of partying was going on, but I only observed. I was sitting outside of a bakery that fed late night hungry drunks. It was about midnight now and Paris was into full force. While I stood observing, a woman rode her bicycle in front of me and chained it to the bike rack. She consumed my attention immediately; beautiful; the elegant kind. She was medium in all sizes. Her hair was brown and shiny and she wore it loosely pulled back. It curved downward over her ears then back upward toward the knot in the back. Her other ear was showing. She looked pleasant as she walked into the bakery alone. I watched her inside the brightly lit bakery through the front windows. The line was long and I had a lot of time to think of what I might say to her. That's the worst scenario; whatever you say is certain to sound like it was created for the situation; fake. I don't know why I was even thinking about this stuff. I only knew English. I'd forgotten.

She came out the door with a loaf of bread. She put it in the basket of her bike and knelt down to unlock her chain. I was watching her every move. But she caught me. She looked up saw me watching. I was frozen in my footsteps. But she spoke:

'Bonjour,' and smiled. 'Bonjour' I smiled back at her. She began situating the chain lock to her bike for departure. She was all loaded up and sitting on her seat ready to pedal off. It was my last chance, so I walked quickly beside her and said the first thing that came to mind:

'Hi, I'm Jesse'

'I did not think you were French'

'How did you know?'

'I've never seen anyone that looked' she paused a moment 'more American than *you*'

Her English was very good, I was in luck.

'What does American look like?

'You'

I goofed on my talking skills and let us sit in a moment of silence, which usually would have given a woman in a situation like this room to say goodbye and pedal off, but instead she said:

'Are you alone?'

'Yes.'

'Would you like to sit somewhere and have a drink with me?'

'Sure' I said, delighted.

'Good. You look strong; you drive us'

'How?'

'Like this' and she showed me.

She sat in the seat while I pedaled the bike standing up. She held onto my waist. We were moving now.

'Tell me where to go' I said.

'I know just the place'

I got squiggly and she laughed, and so did I. It was fun.

'Wait, what is your name?' I turned around and looked at her while we coasted down a slight hill.

'Anya!' she said smiling big.

Anya appeared to be about thirty. That was almost ten years older than me. After five or ten blocks she directed me to stop and we locked her bike. We ended at an outdoor café on a main Paris intersection. I remember it to be a round-about with constant traffic. As we looked out from the cafe, I also remember seeing a large statue that stood in the middle of the road as traffic swarmed around it.

'Are you from Paris?'

'Yes, I have lived here my entire life'

The waitress came. I didn't dare to order in English, so I asked Anya, 'Will you please order me a coffee?'

'So, what brings you to Paris?'

'It's in the way of London'

She liked my joke.

'Actually, I have been travelling much of Europe for a long time, now.'

'You are by yourself?'

'I am'

'How sad; you have no friends or a woman, maybe?'

'I wanted to travel alone. Besides, no one would like to travel the way I do.'

Here I told her some stories that would impress her. I think they did. I love when a person seems genuinely interested in a story you tell.

'How old are you, Anya?'

'I am forty two'

'And you?'

'Twenty one'

'You are so young! But you behave much older.'

Our coffees came.

'You have no children - no husband?'

'Nothing but a father who lives on the other side of Paris – and friends, of course.'

'Why not, can I ask?'

'I never found a man who I was truly in love with. I would not settle for less. But I am still not finished searching, although I am so old, you know.'

'You're just warming up.'

It took her a second to compute the expression.

'Are you not lonely travelling so long by yourself?'

Considering the situation, the answer to this question was obvious.

'I am very lonely. But I only realized it recently'

'How sad; when will you go home?'

'Soon. I am headed there now.'

'How will you get there?'

'I am going to try and make a boat when I get to the beach' I said with a serious, serious expression. She definitely believed me for the brief moment before she laughed.

'Really, but what will you do?'

'I want to see only one more place, that's all: Omaha beach'

'*Normandy?*' she switched to a French accent.

'Yes, Normandy'

'Ah, it is very far, you should know.'

'It's ok'

'Are you not scared?'

'I do get scared sometimes...'

'But you have so much courage, which I like. Not so many people have this.'

'Thanks'

'Are you a Christian?'

I paused a while.

'Are you?'

'No. I have never believed in God.'

'Did you go to church?'

'Never. My father does not believe in God.'

'I always went to church.'

'That is good.

'Ya.'

We were both finished our coffees.

'Shall we go?'

'Where?'

'It is a beautiful night; would you like to ride the bicycle more? I will show you some of Paris if you would like.'

'I would,' and smiled, standing from my seat.

Anya and I rode the bike a hundred blocks that night, as if I hadn't had enough exercise. But I overcame my exhaustion for the sake of... fun. She even brought me to Antoine Street. Anya and I had a surreal connection together; one which age difference could not cheaply steal from us. Many times, we walked next to the bike so we could have better conversation. We were on many crowded streets and enjoyed observing the people together. That is why she was on her bike in the first place. It's what she likes to do at night for pleasure.

'It is so nice to have someone to do this with, Jesse. I have ride my bike many nights alone.'

She didn't know how to say ride in the past tense.

'I've traveled Europe as many nights alone.'

We turned down some avenues away from all the people. We were alone on a street lined with deserted vehicles and dim apartments. Ahead of us, yellow street lights put a distinctive and memorable glare on the scene. I walked the bike on my left side. Anya was on my right. We didn't have anything more to say at the moment, walking silently for many minutes. But I must add, it wasn't uncomfortable in anyway. In an unexpected attempt to break the silence, Anya softly slid her hand into my palm. There's nothing like holding a strangers hand for the first time. It fit exceptionally well, which I think each of us could feel. I didn't give recognition to it immediately, but then I did look at her and we smiled together.

'It is art, no?'

'It is art, Anya' I said sincerely, 'But are we the artists or the artwork?'

'I believe we are the work.'

'I believe *so*.'

Later that night, lying against Anya in her bed, she asked me something in a serious tone.

'Jesse?'

'Yes?'

'Has God been speaking to you?'

Everything inside of me stopped for a moment, then rebooted to normal performance and raced furiously to compensate for its faltering pause. This question was beyond coincidence. She didn't even believe in God.

'What - did you say?' I asked sternly, so I could be reassured my senses heard her properly.

'Does God speak to you? He does not speak to me. I wish he would.'

'No, Anya, you asked has God *been* speaking with me. That means something different.'

'Oh, I did not mean it. Do you speak with God?'

CHAPTER 14

Anya and I spent the next afternoon together. We walked Notre Dame and the Eiffel Tower; the romantic things. We parted at dinner time. She was going away on business, but we each promised to keep in touch. I haven't talked to her since. I didn't like beginning a new journey into the night, so I figured I would find a cozy place to sleep and leave when the sun first showed itself.

It took me a long time to find the train station where I left my pack inside a locker, but I finally did. Walking around, perusing Paris, the day went along unbelievably fast and I hadn't even scouted a proper place to sleep. I hadn't seen a spot that looked all too safe. I remembered seeing some canals earlier in the day. There were bridges that crossed them. I learned quickly in Europe how the underside of a bridge is a brilliant place for sleep. I was likely to be left alone there, so I began retracing my steps to find what I had seen. Navigating unfamiliar cities became second nature to me. When I finally found them, the night had grown well into the dark. It took some climbing and maneuvering to get underneath the bridge, but I had success in seconds. It would be much more difficult to get back up to the city streets, however. The waterway, which now, was running right beside my feet, was encompassed by high concrete walls.

Just as I heaved my pack onto my back and walked toward the bridge, I looked and at once saw that the spot was occupied by several people. They were all staring at me. I wasn't sleeping next to bums. I don't trust bums. There was another bridge one hundred yards up stream, so I made my way towards it. I would have to walk through the occupied space, however. I couldn't see what sort of people they were. I was most concerned about younger men who might be ambitious enough to attack me. When there isn't a soul in the world that knows your whereabouts, or a person on this side of the Atlantic ocean that gives a damn about you, one really begins to develop certain instincts for survival; eyes in the back of your head, per se. The more nights a man closes his eyes alone, the more instinctual he becomes. Look at the bums.

A bum stood in the narrow walkway of level concrete where I needed to pass. To his right was inclined concrete that led up to the steel of the bridge where others sat. It was distinctly darker under the bridge and the lights above created a definitive shadow-line, which the man standing was just tucked comfortably within. To walk through was an intimidating concept for me, but hesitation could have ultimately led to my demise, so I was certain not to show any of it. I never redirected my initial glance; only started walking. I brushed by the bearded man standing in the way and watched his white eyeballs look at me in a slow-motion-pass. I showed him the whites of my eyes too. Once I passed by him I looked up into the ascent on my right and studied the ones sitting. They were quiet. It wasn't a big bridge, so I was almost to the other side. But right as I was about to breech the shadow-line, I heard someone speak in a singing sort of manner:

'Akadubiak'

It sounded like it was directed at me, so I slowed and looked just over my shoulder out of the corner of my eye.

'I see it... Yuh' got that Akadubiak.'

It was English; or so I thought.

'Excuse me?' I said with my body still halfway turned away.

It was a woman's voice with a strong Southern American drawl; Tennessee area around North Carolina, I guessed; I know my American dialects. There was an undulating tone in the speaker's voice. The words sounded as if they escaped from the depths of homeless insanity.

'The soul who spends a night in hell will never awaken' she replied.

'What!?' I scowled. I was tired and irritable.

'Yuh' ain't in hell yet, don't worry.'

Okay. She had my attention. I opened my shoulders and faced her, then took one step.

'No such thing as *hell*,' I said.

'But thought you was in it for a minute there.'

'Yes – it's hard to tell what's real these days. What's your name, Mam?'

'Arthesta Pucket. It *is* a pleasure.'

'I'm Jesse Antoine – good to meet you.'

'Ain't no place like home, boy, but yuh' probably don't need told - if I had to guess.'

'No. No I don't. So what were you saying, I have the Akadubiak?'

With the light available from the end of the bridge, the right side of her face had a darker hue over it. She looked old; late seventies probably. She wore full length clothing that I couldn't much make out.

'It's the sickness you got.'

'Oh? And what's that?'

'Yew ought tuh' know. Sickness is in the soul, son.'

'No. It's bacteria or cancer that gets inside your body.'

'I suppose they'as bacteria and disease floatin' round, but they only attack a weakened spirit, I can assure you.'

'Well, I feel just fine.'

She was obviously crazy, and I was in no mood for a crazy person right now.

'You not the only one get's antsy *livin*'.

'I'm patient' I reasoned with her.

'Than why yuh' under a briudge?'

'For sleep.Why are you?'

'Dogs and cats'

'Dogs and cats…' I returned sarcastic and frustrated.

'Ever owned a dog or cat?'

'A dog'

'God's greatest parody on earth; he's up there gettin' a big laugh out o' it right now.'

'I don't understand what you're talking about, Mam.'

'That Plato talks about the nature of man, don't he?… but I'm tellin' you right now, it's simple as that; dogs n' cats.'

I started listening closer.

'They'as only two types of people in this world; they'as the dogs and then there's the cats. They'as the loyal sort; dependable as can be - the ones that let you get tuh' know them; *them* is written all over their faces. Then they'as the ones yuh' cayn't never fully trust. Yuh' cayn't never fully understand or know them. Although some never will, there's always the chance they'll turn on yuh' without rhyme or reason. And what do yuh' know? Us humans got em' livin' in our own homes; lovin' on em' and what have you. God's a-laughing, alright.

'How interesting' I thought. 'Why are you here? How did you get to be under this Bridge Miss Arthesta?'

'Had me that same Akadubiak, I guess. After the communists and the bankers took over the government with the New Deal and we entered the war to end all wars, I saw changes startin' tuh' happen. Everything went awry. People started losin' sight of things.'

'Like what?'

'Well,' she paused a while to think and look around, 'It all started with the money. Men started losin' even the most basic business principles; they couldn't even realize the effect of doin' a good deed no more.'

I knew for certain Arthesta had lost some serious brain cells, or social skills over the years under that bridge, and only god knows what else, but I also started realizing she was deeper - there was a real authentic story behind her. The more she spoke, the more interesting she became. I sat beside her, uninvited, on the cold concrete. It didn't seem to faze her. I kept my eye on the others – didn't want to be scammed here, still. She always looked away as she spoke. I wandered what in her past caused such a behavior. With Arthesta, you had to be real patient and decipher what she was talking about most of the time, but if you did, it often all came together for a most desirable outcome:

'All a business-man needs to do is give his customer something for free one single time. But it has to be unconditional, don't forget. Whether it be an extra quarter lb. of turkey or a half-off box of nails; whatever says 'I appreciate you coming to see me,' and from that day forward, that customer will go out of his way to return the favor. Stick your neck out for another and you'll see a neck stick out an inch futha'.'

I was struck by the sheer truth of it. She stopped a brief moment, then continued:

'Don't seem like much, but this little thing can go on forever.'

'Like how?'

'Well, I'll tell yuh how.' It's the *whole* idea behind a community. It's the thing that starts one and continues one. America lost it because everything tried to get too damned big - including the government. Ain't no different here; guess I'm a damned fool.'

'You are definitely not a fool. Where are you from, Arthesta?' I asked patiently,
sounding much like a teacher would to a young child. It was difficult to keep her on track and I wanted more story.

'That's a whole nuther' story, boy. Italians are just niggers turned inside out. Oops, I forgot I ain't loud to say that no more, but nevermind it, they said my daddy had some I-talian blood inim, so that makes me loud to say it. Yuh' ain't I-talian are yeuh?' she asked turning at me and staring in my eyes for the very first time.

'No, I'm French and Irish, I guess. Mostly American, though.'

'French!? Why, you don't look French none. What's your last name?'

'Antoine'

'Damned, that sounds I-talian! You sure you ain't I-talian?'

'I'm positive I ain't I-talian. But, Arthesta! I want you to tell me how you got here – and why?'

'Life's a cantankerous thing, I'll tell yeuh. Ain't you ever felt before, like you was meant for more than what they got us lined up for? A bigger purpose than what they make people do? I cayn't explain it – it's just a fact. It's that same reason your dreams come true sometimes. I just weren't made for wastin' the precious life. I was meant to feel the sun shine and to feel that wonderful breeze hit my face every day.'

'I sure like that breeze too.'

'No sir, they couldn't trick me into it. Guess you're starting to see it too.'

'What?'

'*Damnit* boy!?' she said sounding legitimately disappointed in me.

'Uh,' I stuttered.

'That freedom.' she said at a whisper, with a finger pointing up to the underside of the bridge.

'I can't think of too many folks who think freedom is life under this bridge'

'How they know what its like if they ain't done it yet?' she continued at a low tone.

'You just know something everyone else in the world doesn't, I suppose.'

'May, my, my – now your speakin' my language. And I suppose you know someone that wouldn't agree with us?'

'You're darn right I do.'

'Who?'

'We could start with my family – then the rest of the world, besides those guys over there.'

'They Christian folk?'

'My family? They are. Yes.'

'Then I'll bet they know a man don't need no big things – lord on your side and all; you'll get the next meal - don't got to worry about that. But whoever don't agree with us, you just do me a favor, boy, and don't let anyone make ya forget what ya seen or done or know – ever. Yew a man yet? er' still a boy?'

'I don't know? A man. How long have you been here in France?'

She was in control of this conversation; not a thing I could do about it.

'Yet you're not certain about it.' she stated.

'Well, Mam,' I tried to be polite and calm her so she would stay focused. 'No one ever really acknowledged me as a man before – that I can remember'

'Ye' daddy never?'

'Never.'

'Eyes ain't just a way of lookin' out yuh' know; they're a better use to look in. And I seen just a man.'

I took a moment to intake what she said to me. I enjoyed it.

'And whether you're a man or not is up to you -- when you decide you are. Ain't up to no one else.'

'A man it is.'

'I reckon we'll make your right of passage right here, then – making it to the other side of this here bridge. You trucked right on by us crazy folk, like something' wrong with you too, and not even a second thought about it, did ya?'

'I haven't made it yet.'

'Best get on your way then, hadn't yuh'?'

'I best.'

'Get on it!' she said – indicating she wasn't looking for a goodbye with anyone.

And so I got on – and breeched the other end of that bridge, immediately feeling the yellow street lights from far above hit me in the face, like I walked right through the pearly gates. Sometimes a sudden change of light at night is a good thing in a situation like mine. It reminds you everything is real – that you're awake. But, in truth, the real story of me and Arthesta was much longer than what I've described. I gave you the most round-about summary one could possibly make. She kept on and on about different subjects and I learned a lot about her past. But like she said, that was a whole new story – one I might tell another day. Our conversation was so long, that by the time I got to passing my right-of-passage, the night had gallivanted-on a good while, and I determined the sleep I'd get underneath any bridge wasn't really sleep worth getting at all, so I headed out of town, Paris that is.

Exiting a big city like that takes strategy, which is more difficult if you have no map and don't speak French. I decided the easiest way would be to take the subway out of town to the farthest stop it would go and, with some luck, I might land myself in a fairly safe residential area with a hint of morning traffic to take me in the direction I was headed: Normandy and Omaha beach. I'd grown up hearing about this place. When I was a little boy staying with my grand pop, I remember watching two things: WWII documentaries and John Wayne. Since I was so close, I thought it was my American duty to pay the respects due. After a grueling process of deciphering French subway maps and interpreting how to get West, I thought I had it figured out. But when it's in another language, you're never certain. I finally got onto, what I thought to be the right train and went along for the ride. As soon as I got on, the conductor spoke several sentences in French. As the train wheels made their first metal to metal revolution below my feet, the conductor started speaking, so right away I got to thinking about what he may be saying: 'Hello ladies and gentlemen, thank you for riding with us today on the Eastbound Route' or 'Bonjour, you have boarded the City-Loop Route, terminating for the night at the current stop.' Either would have been a nightmare.

Paris subways are suspicious in the afternoon, so you need to use your imagination pretty well to picture me here at the earliest hours of morning. My train was rusted and rickety. I was alone on it until the first stop, where a residentially challenged man walked on and sat in the isle beside me. He looked over at me, therefore, I could determine he was not one of the 'no-talk' bums. We had a talker! I didn't feel overly safe, to say the least. I sat in a more prepared, aggressive position when several more drunks walked through the aisle.

I needed countryside. The city exhausted me fast. I don't seem to be made for the city. I was beginning to feel the wear of the many nights and long roads behind me. I barely gave the Eiffel Tower a second glance. I hardly had the energy to navigate my course, so I more or less was at the point of riding the train aimlessly like the rest of the bums, just hoping for some outside visuals to give me an idea when to exit, but then again, I still cannot tell what those people are thinking when I look at them.

The inside of the train cabin was extremely bright. When the dark of night flattened the other side of the window, it combined and contrasted to create a perfect reflection of myself. I hadn't seen my face for a while. I hadn't ascertained the reasonable opportunity to stop and look. It was quite pale with dark circles around my eyes. I tilted my ball cap up high so I could examine it closely. I stared right into my eyes for a long time. Meanwhile, my head and body bounced in all directions as a byproduct of the thousands of revolutions per second the metal wheels below my body were making. I searched and asked: Who was I? I tried hard to answer questions. I studied my face and saw an unfamiliar man. I thought deeply on that face. Now, in a staring contest with myself, I intimidated him into a submission of information. In the act, I came out of my body; exposed myself; unveiled my soul into the nude; vulnerable, he and I both became witnesses to truth. One thing we realized is the only truth I deny myself is the truth about myself.

What I was able to do in that moment – to look inward – is the one and only thing that separates man from animal. We must never lose it. Sadly, my trance was interrupted by a stop, whereupon two men entered opening doors. They were younger; around twenty five. They looked poor and drunk, or on drugs – but not quite bums. One was black, one white. They were talking loudly as they came through, but their conversation seemed to suddenly stop as they recognized me and my pack as a foreign object. They sat two rows behind me and across, looking the bum in the back of the head. He didn't mind their presence. They looked at me, but tried to do so inconspicuously, it seemed. I felt possible danger, so I made my own inconspicuous move and stood up after the next stop. I was better preparing myself for an attack. I briefly looked at the maps and read things as if I understood. I was definitely far from the safety of tourist areas, but knew nothing for certain of the area or more importantly, of its safety. It didn't too badly concern me at the time, I'm just telling you now what I knew.

I rode for a good forty minutes on that tram. I was pleased when the tram exited the tunnel system and went above ground. At the third above-ground stop, I decided to make a smart move. As the doors opened I held onto the pole and looked at the ground as if I wasn't concerned with the stop. When the doors made their first movement towards a close, I bolted out and they pinched the back of my pack. I escaped into the dark streets of West Paris – hopefully.

CHAPTER 15

That same morning, the sun was rising and I was walking. My first objective was to find a map and get my bearings. I did this at the first gas station where a helpful man worked with me through hand gestures. I didn't buy the map, but later wished I had. It was only an extra four dollars, but I was thinking of how badly I needed to eat, so I refrained. Instead, I bought a bottle of water, three cookies and a pack of crackers. This would last me until 11am that night – walking. I got myself clear out of the city, which bit a chunk out of my morning, then found the necessary highway to head west toward my destination.

My first ride that day was a middle-aged school teacher. She was brave to give a strange man a ride. It was a valiant and respectable gesture. I made her decision worth while with friendly conversation, trying to make her as comfortable as possible - despite my exhaustion to the point of delirium. Her English was sufficient enough for a good conversation, which was rare in France, but I had found it. She had a daughter exactly my age in University, which was our choice topic. I was truly blessed to have received this ride so soon. It would be one of my last.

We parted ways somewhere between Evreux and Caen – closer to Caen, I think – which left me, if I had to estimate, about 50 miles from my destination. She drove me a considerable distance. The roads after Caen were, for the most part, dead straight. But they were not flat. For a while, a mile at a time, it consistently made dips, up and down, like the waves in the ocean. I reached the top of one hill, only to be greeted by another valley far below, with yet another hill to climb after it, which I could see the top of. I hoped for the landscape to flatten out, but it never did. Luscious, well-groomed farms outlined the road beside me the entire way. The crops were at their peak; blossoming – green – beautiful.

After I passed Caen, there was but one real town on the way to the beaches, which was Bayeux. I passed Caen without even a look, but I stopped for a gander in Bayeux; all-the-while on the lookout for someone headed my same direction. No luck. All the tourists were taking busses to the beaches, and I couldn't budge for that. I was starving by the time I reached the town of Bayeux, but it was touristy with high prices and I hadn't allowed myself to eat food from anywhere but a grocery store in over three months. Due to the divine intervention recently imparted onto my life, I reassured myself I would be provided for wherever I went and so I continued on my trek out of Bayeux without food. The population was sparse and so was car travel. From Caen, I received one ride of about five miles toward Bayeux. After Bayeux, I received, also, only one ride of several miles. I'd say I walked nearly 40 miles in the second half of that day, moving at a grueling pace. I wanted so badly to sleep. Don't forget that I haven't done that in a while. I began thinking of knocking on the door of each farmhouse I passed and asking to rest in their barn. But there was something I wanted even more (to get home), so I pushed myself to keep walking.

After Bayeux, the roads no longer had yellow lines, and became severely winding. Several cars came bustling around the corners, but the ones that did never even considered stopping. I knew I was close, but my curiosity crushed my spirit with each hour added onto my walk, without any signs of my final destination. I expected signs all the way from Paris for tourists searching for the beaches of Normandy, but the French acted like they didn't know what I was talking about, let alone any signs. It seemed like the walking would never end; as if I were in a time-warp – a reality of slow motion. I became frustrated and upset. I thought I would have to relinquish the fight for the Atlantic that day.

The day was on its way out - still here, but backing out of the driveway. I was approaching a sharp bend in the now narrow road. Pine trees suddenly surrounded me in this particular spot. I don't know why, but I have an oddly vivid recollection of this moment. The bend in the road seemed to pass extraordinarily slowly. My steps didn't seem to be advancing my position. I thought how fun it would be to feel the inertia of taking this turn in a car. But this thought only exacerbated the sluggishness of time, granting me the ability to understand the agonizing anticipation in the life of a turtle.

As I was exiting the bend on the other side, I passed by a picnic bench tucked underneath some pine trees on my right side. There were no clear indications, but it seemed to be for public use.

I then turned my attention to the sky, which was crammed tightly with one single grey cloud. It was low to the ground and I felt it pressing down on my shoulders. With those big trees surrounding me, I felt the day's first shift in temperature towards colder. From then-on, the air steadily cooled. I thought of what bad shape I would be if it started raining, so I needed to consider shelter now. There was maybe an hour left until dusk, and there were no signs of how close I was to my destination, so I reluctantly decided to give up the fight and crawled underneath the picnic table with soft, dead yellow pine needles bedding the ground and I shut my eyes.

I rolled from side to side without sleep. Minutes later a car zoomed by and rustled me in several ways. I was angry with my decision to give up the search for the beach, so with a motivating pissed off attitude, I threw my pack from underneath the table, crawled out, stood up straight, lowered my grumpy brow over my eyes, heaved my pack onto my shoulders and stomped-on forward. I walked for another twenty minutes and still found no beach. God, I could smell the Ocean air, where was it?

I came upon a small community with several newly built homes. There was not much activity there – certainly not a store, which reminded me of the hunger in my stomach. I could hardly continue; I needed food to nourish my overused legs from walking and my back and shoulders from carrying that heavy pack. As I entered this small community of homes, just off the road was a naked cinder block frame to an unfinished house. It looked like a great shelter; a place I could really get some rest in. As I stood there considering it, a drop of rain struck the topside of my hand. I wobbled up to the structure through the mounds of hard dirt, freshly bulldozed. I leaned against the blocks at the entranceway and looked in, then looked back out to consider who might be watching. Then I checked the sky again. After a minute or two of contemplation, I left that nice shelter behind with an uncertain determination. The sky was threatening darkness. A dim hue had nestled its way into the atmosphere. I just let go of my mind and walked more.

Within a mile, a man was tinkering about his yard on my left. He was the first soul I had seen outside of a car. I walked up his nice driveway and said 'Misseur, pardon muah...The Beach?' He studied me confused for a second.

'Ahhh - the beach' he smiled,' pointing his index finger beside his head in an act of declaration. Then he ran inside.

He returned with car keys and signaled me to come with him. The man drove me several miles to the beach. 'Merci bocou,' I said many times, 'Thank you very much,' I repeated with graciousness. There's no way I would have made it before dark. I jumped out of the car and walked about one hundred yards in the direction he pointed. I found myself standing atop a great hill of sand -- overlooking the Atlantic Ocean. The cloud cover ended just short of the horizon, which granted me the clear privilege of watching the sun honorably concede to the infringing darkness. I collapsed to my knees as I saw it. The horizon was mine once again. I had seized it as my own. My eyes never faltered from the display. I gazed steadily, as if hypnotized. I was in the appropriate position on my knees as I accepted his warmth and his ancient wisdom.

When it was over, I navigated myself with careful steps down the steep grade to visit the water. I walked along the shore into the encroaching night. Each wobbly step I took saw an inch more of darkness. I saw no one. Nothing was around. There were no trees for me to even sleep under. I was isolated by the tall, barren hill to my left. Feeling the chilly wind come off the Ocean, I feared that the rain was coming. I thought of the soldiers who may have landed in the spot I stood. It humbled me. It made me feel sad, yet fortunate. War is an experience millions upon millions of men before me have witnessed and understood. For that reason, I am inferior to them; I lack what seems to be part of my nature – as though I am deprived of the earliest practice of manhood; deprived of the chance to witness man's one truly authentic capability. In fact, I was created more for the ability to fight than I was for the use of reason. I don't struggle to develop civility or to use logic or reason, I struggle to maintain those things against the constant brink of war that I daily stand upon. I can never back away from it. I never will. No man ever does. But with the development of my mind, I know I can stand on that cliff's edge for a lifetime without falling, and so, I am thankful for my deprivation.

I walked about a mile - to where I saw a white van sitting in the darkness right on the beach. I only saw complacency around it from the distance, but as I approached closer, I realized two people were sitting on the other side. I intentionally steered myself closer to get a better look. I looked at them as I walked by and said 'Bonjour.' They each replied, then indicated for me to come over with a hand gesture. I did. It was a young French couple. Their English was limited, but we worked it out just fine. The man was a truck driver and I forget what she did. I sat and talked with them. They shared some drinks of vodka with me, and the best thing of all: **a ham dinner with potatoes and baked beans.**

Over dinner, I was inquiring of their knowledge of a place I could sleep. The man indicated he knew of something up the hill. The alarming sound of rain came from just above the hill and ended our little party. A moment after we heard it, sure enough, that rain hit us with a force comparable to its sound. The man quickly let me borrow a flashlight to go find whatever it was I needed to find up the hill, but my expression must have been one of confusion, so he grabbed the flashlight and took off up the hill in a run to show me. I followed right behind him. We dodged around big dry-like sand bushes. In the brief minutes of running up the hill, I went into a daydream of storming the beach as a soldier. I imagined being shot at and my fellow Americans dropping to the ground all around me. But about three quarters up the hill, the man stopped and pointed the light down into a hole in the ground. I knew what it was immediately - a remnant Nazi bunker. I didn't want to, but I had no choice whatsoever; the rain had come down on me so hard, I was drenched as if jumping into a swimming pool: clothes wet to the skin. It was that hard of a rain, indeed. The man went running back to his van, taking his flashlight along with him. That's okay; I had my own flashlight: the kind that's the size of a human fingernail and goes on a keychain. The wind coming off the Ocean was strong and cold and brought instant chills to my wet bones. I stuck my head in first and tried to look around. The thunder was vibrating the earth, which made my instinct for shelter even more pressing. Shining my little light inside, I thought I could make out a concrete floor. I hoped nothing lived in there.

CHAPTER 16

I dropped my pack in first and waited a moment... Nothing. So I lowered myself down with my hands hanging onto the brim of concrete above and dropped to my feet. I flicked on my fingernail-size light and it allowed me to see a solid one foot ahead. I searched the perimeter, walking slowly. It was a concrete room that was either dilapidated with time, or crippled from an American grenade. It smelled rampant with feces. I could hear the bat's return to home, curious who their new visitor was. I dug into my bag and changed, in the dark, into a dirty t-shirt and pair of jeans far too many times worn. I chose a far corner and laid down on my side in the fetal position and tried to rest. I shivered from the cold air that finagled its way down the opening, where it continued over to my corner, blowing down my shirt-collar, as if there were a person quivering their lips and exhaling a cold winter's breath on me. My eyes were open and I stared into the blackness with fear.

I only shut my eyes a few times, shivering into the night. I felt things crawling on me, but that was the least of my worries. I was too tired to think, but kept thinking. I thought about home; about how badly I wanted to be home. I knew I wouldn't sleep any, which would make three in a row. And I was truthfully concerned about having the sheer physical ability to drag myself out of this place. As long as it had taken me to get to the beaches, it would take me to get out, and my feet were throbbing from today's walk alone. I was legitimately worried for myself. There was no one in the world looking after me; not a soul who cared. It was up to me alone. I closed my eyes with this thought in mind and shook my head left and right -- furious as to how I got myself in such a predicament.

This is going to be difficult for me to say. I don't quite know how to present it, actually, but here it is - plane and simple: I began to hear things that night -- abnormal things. I studied the ubiquitous blackness, trying to locate the sounds, but the more I looked, the darker I perceived it to be. Each time I heard it, I tried to bury my backside deeper into the cold concrete wall, but it didn't stop the chills from running like spiders down my neck. These were the worst kind of chills -- chills created by the purest, most genuine and instinctual feeling of fear combined with an already shivering body whose only warmth was coming from the chilled concrete walls of a damp cave. It wasn't human voice I heard – I know this. It wasn't anything animal either, nor the sound of the ocean, nor of the air. Whatever was in there with me, I do know, was directing its frenzy at my presence.

The sounds intermittently ceased, but I was still tense during that time, waiting for them to return. I hadn't heard it for maybe thirty or forty minutes. I would have left the cave if the noise hadn't been coming from the direction of my only exit. I was far too frightened to approach such a thing. Instead, I stayed and hoped for daybreak. I wished for it with all of my might. I thought hard for the earth's revolution to speed up – just for me; that, or for my sense of time to speed up; either would have been fine.

However bad this was, I would have preferred death over the feeling that happened next: a different noise entirely. Something heavy – like a man – dropped to its feet from above where I had entered. It paused for a moment, as if to look around into the blackness just as I had done when I first came in. After that, I heard its first step. I was listening as fiercely as a body could. I honed all of my senses into one single area, where I estimated the noise had occurred -- like a deer in the woods or the mule you ride. In a second's time, I transformed from an exhausted man in a state of delirium, to an all-alert, all-instinctual, all-powerful animal. Its second step was made. It was barely noticeable, but my ears picked-up on the smallest pebble that crunched beneath what was my understanding of a shoe. Next, my ears sharply created an image of a hand running along the concrete wall as another two steps followed. My mind raced like a super computer to analyze every factor: what type of person would be in the same spot as me in the middle of the night, what are the chances of them seeing me, how much danger did this pose, what type of person made that footstep, and whether to be quiet or to speak.

I chose silence. I never moved a muscle -- just waited patiently on my side, with my eyes watching the darkness. The individual took several more steps in my direction, closing in and cornering me. Another step and they would kick my body. This all happened quickly. Just as my lips were engaged to speak, it stopped. I heard them adjacently sliding their back down the concrete wall and I presumed they were in a crouching position when the noise stopped. I heard no movement of the feet sliding out from beneath them. They were within arms reach of me and I still remained silent.

For minutes they stayed in that position, as if considering whether they wished to stay in the cave that night or not. I thought they would never move in those minutes. But they decided to remove their feet from under them into a more comfortable position on their bum, which meant they were staying. I continued to study the situation. I decided I must speak before it goes any farther. So, simultaneously, not remembering I was in France, I simply said 'Hello,' while moving myself into an upright position – but careful not to seem aggressive. I didn't even finish the first word and they were scrambling to their feet in a frantic race toward the exit. At first I didn't say anything, and I wasn't going to. But before they could climb out, I yelled 'Wait! I'm not going to hurt you!'

They stopped and paused exactly where they stood.

'Who are you?' a man's voice came out of the dark space.

'Just a man, sir. I'm only here to get clear of the rain.'

'Well you gave me quite a fright just-a-man.'

'I'm sorry, I tried not to.'

'Can I ask you a question?'

'Yes.'

'*Why in the hell did you not say anything before*!? --Let me damn near creep up and step on you!'

'Because I thought you were following me! Why would you sneak up on a man like that!?'

'Sneak!? I didn't figure for anyone to be situated down in a hole.'

'And I didn't figure for anyone to be creeping up on me while I was situated down in a hole!'

'Fair enough, lad -- you speak English,' he said surprised-like.

'And so do you'

'Well, of course – I invented the language.'

'How'd you do that?'

'I'm English, mate.'

'Fair enough. Come over here if you'd like. I'm no harm to you.'

'I'm bloody glad you mean me no harm. I left my satchel over there next to you.'

He came over and retrieved his satchel. He was in front of me, but I could not see him. I knew I was looking at him. It took me a second, but I realized he was looking back at me. Yet, neither of us could see even the slightest silhouette of the other.

'The name is Jesse.'

'Bill. Bill Stirpoke.'

We fumbled to meet hands on the first pass, but found a good grip of each other on the second. It was a strange reception of another man's hand – and one of the most awkward encounters I've ever had, I can confidently say.

'So what brings you to this here hole?'

'I'm typically a sucker for a wet hole on a rainy night as such. What brings an American into a French hole? Or is it a German hole?'

'I'm at the end of a long journey. This is my last stop, which means, in the morning I'm sorting out how to get home.'

'Ah ha, and you have quite a puddle to jump, compared to mine. I'm also headed for home after a long journey. How life greets you with a companion amidst such a tempest.'

'It's a story for all man, Bill.'

'Who will tell it first?'

'Whoever first finds someone interested to listen.'

'You have a quick wit. Shall we have a sit?'

'Let's.'

And so we sat on the ground, in that same corner I had laid just moments before. I sat upright against one wall, facing the exit, and he sat on the wall to my right, making his line of sight cross mine at a ninety degree angle.

'So…what was the meaning of this journey of yours?' I asked somewhat sarcastically – yet, it was clear I was only inquiring of his prior travel destinations.

'What meaning did I find, or what meaning did I intend on?'

'Tell all.'

'It could take some time, which *you* are running out of.'

'Like all of us are; only, I don't feel it.'

'Funny to hear that.'

'*Is it now?*'

'To answer your question, I started as a sage for my ideas, but found that I've returned a mere story-teller.'

'How do you mean?'

'When your listener only listens, you haven't the wisdom of a sage.'

'What more can they do?'

'Follow me to the end.'

'Where are you going?'

'Not to heaven, I know that much.'

'Where to?'

'If you're asking where the soul goes, just look outside at the ocean – at the waves. The life of a wave is the life of a man. It begins from no where – that *we* know of. It travels long distances to get to the shore; each one a soul. When it's over, they disintegrate into the ground and recycle back around. Look at the plants and trees in late November; limp, lifeless, dead, yet alive - waiting for new life, just around the corner. The seasonal life of a plant is the life of a soul. Death is only a change in seasons, I promise you.'

'But we're different.'

'You aren't. You – man – must evolve now. But this time, not in the direction of bettering himself against nature - in the direction of being it again. It's the only answer; and nature has decided it already. Do you see?'

'Yes. I see. But - I already recycle plastics.'

He paused

'And you prove me a story-teller.'

'No, I prove you a boring sage.'

He paused

'I shouldn't have said that. I'm sorry,' I jumped in before he could speak.

'It's okay, sometimes bugs bite for no reason.'

'They do, damn things. Wait, are you calling me a bug?'

'But people squash the bugs right back. Without reason, of course.'

'No, they squash because bugs bite without cause.'

'How do you know we didn't squash first?'

'Because I called you boring.'

'Who's talking about us?'

'uhhhh…..In that case, I don't, exactly -- but I know if bugs were bigger, they'd squash us too.'

'Exactly; which is why you are a bug.'

'Bzzzzzz,' I buzzed like a bug.

'Want to know how not to be a bug?'

'Bzzzzzz,' I buzzed again.

I honestly didn't think this was real anymore so I just kept buzzing at him, making a joke of what we were talking about, but also in an acceptance of my newly established insanity -- due to the current situation, of course.

'It is easy, Jesse, just don't bite back.'

'Bill, I'll be sure my home is equipped with a fly-swatter in every room.'

'Fine, but one last thing.'

'Go for it.'

'You must understand something.'

'Okay. What?'

'The common realization of strength is fake; the stronger man concedes.'

'So you want me to let the bug bite?'

'Ahhh' he sighed with relief, 'my return to sage-hood… let it bite. It will end the war.'

'Maybe so. But I'm afraid I'm a warsmith and nature has decided it already.'

'There are *some* things out of her reach. *Cogito Ergo Sum.*'

'You said your name was *Bill Stirpoke*?'

'Yes.'

'I don't know why, but… that sounds sort of familiar.'

'Close your eyes for a moment.'

'Do what? It's so dark, I….' I stopped. 'Wait, what for?'

'Chap, just do it,' he interjected.

'Ok.'

'Are they closed?'

'Yes.'

'Now: In your personal and undeniable space of darkness, I want you to search for colors and for movement. And search hard for them, too. They're there.'

I followed his instructions.

'Have you done what I've asked?'

'Yes. I see color.'

'Mate - tell me: amidst this solitary blackness, is what you see a creation of your imagination because I've asked, or is it real?'

I paused for a while to think.

'I think…'

'Don't tell me,' he intervened swiftly. 'It was a question for you only, not for me.'

'A strange one, I'll say. Hey, I thought you had a story to tell.'

'I can - if you fancy stories.'

'I fancy.' I liked his use of that word.

'Let me think a moment.'

So the man began telling a story. To the best I can remember, it went something like this:

On a day and a time, when this world seemed so much more than usual to brightly shine -- when the gloom of a wet winter was winched away by the golden beams of a sun that warmed all the people, and spring time was now the dawn of the day, adventure was on its way.

Beneath the trees that had no leaves, sun beams shot through the forest seams and sparkled off the hair of golden streams of a boy far, far down below. He strolled as carelessly as a young boy would, investigating everything he could.

He poked and prodded, climbed and conquered, discovering unknown crevices all about. He became the king, all alone, of a place no one else knew about. He wandered so far from home, he could shout and shout… neither mom nor dad, nor brother or sister would return his call.

Behind a nearby Oak tree, he noticed a group of squirrels investigating him. In fact, the boy even thought they seemed to be playing peeka-boo, disappearing and reappearing on opposite sides of the tree - at the top and at the bottom, poking their heads in and out. He even thought they were giggling at him. But his curiosity with the squirrels was short-lived and so he continued to walk. . .

He now walked along a creek nearly twenty feet wide, with water that whisked by and by, which is where the boy within the boy started to become sly. He came across a bee hive hanging in a tree. They were hard at work, collecting and building whatever they could, but for whatever reason, with a piece of wood, the boy smacked the hive straight from where it stood.

He laughed and chuckled, but soon would regret this evil-doing. First, one bee buzzed and circled his head, tickling his ear - then two, then three, and now the whole clan was out for revenge. In a frenzy of madness, they flew toward him with stingers out in front. He took off running as fast as his legs could go, with the buzzing noise close on his tail. In an all out run, he took the first visible trail.

He ran long and hard, and when he finally thought he was safe, he stopped, huffing and puffing. He looked around and he recognized nothing. A cold and yucky sweat was now on his head, and his heart pounded hard, while his face turned bright, bright red.

He had been so happy to be far and free from anyone who could tell him how to be. But this beautiful day was on its way out; dusk moving in, without a doubt. The feeling of fright was moving in as quickly as the night. And the worst part of all: he was now lost and alone.

His first mission would be to find the stream. He knew it could lead him home. He listened as closely as he could, and finally heard the water. What a relief, he thought, that he was now on his way. And he followed the stream, which soon brought him back to the place where he knocked down the bee hive. He sprinted quickly past it, making sure not to be seen.

From a distance, a waterfall came into sight. And as soon as he saw it, the clan of bees swarmed by the opposite side of the creek, still, with their stingers forward, apparently in a frenzy. He jumped behind a tree to hide. The waterfall flowed rapidly and he felt its cold air. As he spied on the bees, hugging the tree, to his amazement the clan flew straight through the waterfall and disappeared! He could only think that they must be so angry from what he did, it made them crazy. But with the clan now dead, and no more worries in his head, he continued to walk. . .

But he only took two or three steps, and out from the waterfall popped the swarm of bees! 'How could this be?' he asked. They flew as fast and untouched as he'd ever seen. He thought to himself, was it a dream?

'MATE, ARE YOU PAYING ATTENTION? I can't see your face.'
'I'm with ya, Bill.'

Thus, naturally, as a curious boy would be, he approached the falls, which were about as tall as he. He looked around to see if the bees were gone, and the coast was clear. He then took off his shirt, inhaled as deep as he could, and pushed his head through. With the cold running water pressing on his neck, he opened his eyes and looked.

What he saw, then and there, can only be described as brilliance. It was so brilliant that it changed his life forever.

After a long night, the boy found his way back home. His mother was joyous of his safe return that she wept of a happy feeling. But within moments she grew sad again, as she discovered something was much different about her boy. There was a problem. He would no longer open his eyes. It wasn't that they didn't work; his eyes worked perfectly fine, yet, the mother wept for many years, unable to understand why he would not use his eyes.

He would say, mother *"Do not cry, my eyes still work, but they have seen all that is needed to see."* For, whenever he was asked throughout his life why he would not open the eyes, he would only say *"My mind no longer requires what they offer."*

They tried and tried to get him to use his eyes, but he simply refused. In fact, there were only three times in the rest of his life that he chose to open them. They are as followed:

The first was upon the death of his father. He had not seen his father's face since the day he wondered off into the woods. It was his one and only father and so he longed to see his face just once more. He stood over the casket and slowly opened his lids. It took him a minute to focus once they were opened, but sure and steady, his vision returned, allowing him to study the face of the man who brought him life. No one had even noticed.

The second was on the wedding day of his son. He opened his eyes just as he heard *"you may kiss the bride,"* where his vision slowly but surely returned and he patiently watched. He closed them immediately after the kiss ended. It was the family he had created which he was so interested to see -- just as his father did before him. And, again, no one had noticed.

He was an old, old man the last time he opened his eyes. He was taking a walk with his wife. They never let go of each other's hand during this walk. It was a sunny day and he could feel the warmth on his face. The wind was blowing powerfully - caressing him like a mother's hand. He heard the wind bustling through the trees beside him which created a beautiful song. The magical feelings from his other senses sparked his curiosity something terrible, so he opened his eyes and sure and steady, his vision returned. He slowly focused in on the trees that were jumping about, making a whisking song. He watched and it brought him great pleasure. When the wind stopped, he directed his eyes briefly toward his wife, who was smiling the brightest smile of her life. He looked into her. At last, he turned his head upward toward the sun and looked into its heart. He watched *and smiled until his vision was taken from him forever. And he smiled more.*

When it was over, he said to his wife: "When will the new human come, my dear? I dream for the day they free themselves. Until it happens just like that; just like a single stroke of mother's windy hand, where in one moment, every man and woman alive can see and think like the greatest men of history, will we continue to sit in the same rooms, or in the same seat, or stand in the same building most of our known lives - in a place that is hell as much we should venture to know; where the sound of telephones ring in our sleep, televisions flash behind our mind, and the humming of some machine is life's musical backdrop; will we sit, dull – remain anxiously satisfied, leaving our ears attentive to this world while the deepest tunnels of our mind wander off to a better place; numb to the truth, mummies in a tomb, idle of conscious, awake for truth.."

After the story Bill stood up and said, "My friend: by the equity in every soul, and that which is vested in me, I declare myself free. No entity, no man, shall ever decree upon me any limitation of land; for I will peaceably roam where I wish. To let the birds approach superior laws or orders – they being free to perch where they desire? I refute that notion and I petition against that style of order; I am free. My solution – the alternative: *chaos*; if this so be the term used to describe subsequent occurrences. Only those afraid of the laws of nature deny my design: that the strong overpower the weak. So one animal is stronger than another; let it be; I hereby accept my death – if, I am free. I wish you to sleep well. I wish you to be free. And above all, I wish for you - knowledge.

I never saw Bill's face. The sun nearly entered as he left and I stayed up for good.

CHAPTER 17

I was at the doorway of my childhood home. People were inside, yet the door was locked. That's the world, I guess: beautiful little families locked away in their safe little chambers. I grabbed the key that lay right where it always was and I realized the feeling it gave me (of familiarity) had become unfamiliar. I entered quietly and walked through the kitchen. It was glowing with cleanliness and a welcoming feeling. Someone had been living a nice life there all this time. It made me feel as though I missed out on a lot of living, which, in reality was probably only work, eat, movie, sleep, repeated monotonously, but nonetheless: amongst family. I passed through the kitchen and stood in the archway of the living room. The TV was on, playing the cartoon Tom and Jerry. I watched the cat chase the mouse for a moment before I realized someone was sitting in the big, red reclining chair in front of me. It was such a large chair that I wasn't able to see a head, so I took a step forward and there sat my grandfather with his hands folded in his lap, peacefully taking a nap while his favorite cartoon played. My step disturbed him and his eyelids opened calmly, not alarmed in the least. He looked at me and said my name in a quiet, vaguely surprised voice:

"Jess."

I replied, "Hey Pop" in a humbled voice.

'Swim back?'

'Yep. Swam.'

'Was the wooder wet?'

'You could say that,' I smiled at the joke he's told all my life.

'See anything worth seein'?

'Not hardly.' A response you could expect from *him* if *he* were asked.

'They went out for a walk. I guess they'll be back soon.'

'Aight Pop.'

I went into my bedroom, which was left exactly the same as the day high school ended. I threw my pack in a corner and laid myself down on my bed, staring at the ceiling. I hadn't moved a muscle for a while when I heard the front door open and a bustle of people coming through. I knew the dog would find me first. I heard her paws running on the hardwood floors in a romp of excitement from her walk. I heard a few familiar voices, then no sooner was the dog standing on chest, going for my face with that sloppy tongue. While I wrestled with her, I heard several footsteps end at the doorway of my room. When I looked, there stood my mother, father, grandmother, and brother all crowded in the little opening, each with the same little grin on their face.

"Hey Bub," my dad said in a deep voice.

"Hey hawney," my grandma said in the super slow motion of a North Carolina accent.

"Yo dude," my brother said carelessly.

My mom came to me first with a little grin and sat on my bed, forcing the dog aside. She put her arm on my shoulder not saying a word.

I didn't know how to act. I was different in so many ways, but I didn't want them to know; people can't quite understand when someone has changed and they weren't there for it. Once you get the inkling to start thinking different, you can't never get it out, either. I'd experienced, among many things, a long lost nomadic freedom that most of humanity lost long ago, and I decided I'd never give it up for anything; that would be my life forever and nothing would get in the way.

A proper country dinner was being fixed right away. Everyone was hungry; me the most. I set the table as people were getting showers and tending to their quick business. I asked around what everyone wanted to drink and filled several glasses with milk, soda and iced tea. All six of us where present at the table and we began eating.

"So you going to tell us about your trip?" someone started.

"Absolutely. What would you like to know?"

"Don't you have any stories to tell?"

"Stories? Not really. I just saw a bunch of stuff."

"Like what?"

"Well, I went to the Eiffel Tower. That was really neat. I saw the beaches of Normandy. I toured a bunch of great cities across Europe and saw lots of beautiful art and architecture. I climbed mountains in Germany, Ireland and Poland, too."

"Didn't you meet any friends or anything?"

"Yes. I traveled with a few people; some whom I hope to keep in contact with."

"Them Europeans treat yeuh okay? I heard they was *ru*de," my grandmom asked.

"Oh yes, they were great. They're just like us grandma."

"Didn't yeuh starve to death over there?"

"Oh no, the food was great. I tried all the foods from every country. I really ate well."

Which was a lie, but I didn't lose weight because the food wasn't any good.

"Didn't you get lonely?"

"I hardly thought about it."

'Where the hell'd ya sleep?'

'Ahhh. Anywhere. I found places.'

'Sounds *re*-tarded to me' my dad emphasized; 'coulda' been home makin' money all that damn time.'

'Coulda been,' was my well programmed response to him.

'Well you missed the Phillies. Man, I'll tell you, they've been on fire. They're going to be a dynasty.'

'Oh ya? That's *great*,' I said with enthusiasm.

We continued conversation about the Phillies for a while, then to a new subject, and then to another, enabling me to withhold the anyways, very unexplainable truth.

CHAPTER 18

Freedom was swiftly sucked from my soul. I returned to normality and it left me only as a set of bones drowning in a feeling of emptiness. I drug myself out of bed to some job, so I could pay my contributions to society: that is, relinquishing my wages for taxes and adding my share of smog to the air as I waited in the lines of daily traffic with my fellow humanoids. I just don't seem to be able to live by the hour or minute hands of a clock, only the increment of one life, which, I am always aware of its time. One of those beautiful afternoons in traffic I became furious with myself, realizing the nauseating truth: I'll never accept society, yet I'll never deny it. The tension of the two forces rang and rang in my head persistently enough for me to decide against the life that was being painted for me, so I packed my bags and left.

There was an old farm high in the mountains of Appalachia where my other grandmother was raised. The property, along with a 100 year-old house remained in the family and I headed straight for it. I drove six hours late in the night. I never do drives like that in the day – I won't sit in traffic – I can't think of a bigger waste. The drive was south-west from the Philadelphia area; mostly west.

The unending sound of my engine on the interstate put me into a trance. That, and the dark night made me groggy. I was half thinking deeply, half not thinking at all. There was no music -- it was a more serious mood than that; I was about to make a life-change. Opposing headlights passed at a perfect four minute interval, which put me under deep hypnosis. I had to stop for gas at some point. There wasn't much to choose from at such a late hour, so I took the first exit that showed signs of life. I was near the end of my travel.

I pulled into the station, where, looking out my window, I slowly cruised past several parked semi trucks. Their interior lights were turned off and I presumed men were in a deep slumber inside. It reminded me of the many nights I spent overseas in truck-stops trying to negotiate rides with similar men, only ones who spoke a different language than me. Before I parked my own car, ten different overseas truck-stops, where I was lost, cold, wet, scared, or hungry slid across my mind like a roll of film.

I exited my vehicle and found myself blitzed by bright lights and the commotion of loud trucks at idle. A loud conversation carried-on overtop the diesel engines. Such a stark change from the safe, peaceful cockpit of my car slightly disturbed my hypnosis for a moment, but it didn't terminate it altogether – I was still dazed as I entered the bright store. It was so bright that nothing seemed real. The bell jingled as the door closed shut behind me and I saw a line of three people standing at the register, so I headed to the bathroom first. It was three a.m. and I don't wait in lines.

I went right up to the urinal and gazed into the wall. There was some rustling-around in the stall beside me, but nothing to be alerted by. I heard someone speaking, but couldn't understand and didn't really listen, either. When they came out, I stood at the urinal still. They move to the sink right beside me – a Chinese man and his five year old son. They spoke to each other quietly. It was, after all, 3am, so I assumed they were also on a long travel. I studied them intensely in that few moments I had. I watched them through the mirror. The father noticed me watching and we nodded at each other and looked away. He quietly conversed with his son in English. The boy was asking a lot of questions. The father's English was extremely poor. I believe he switched languages out of courtesy for me. When he did this, I was overcome with an equally humble appreciation for his respect. His attempts at my language, however poor, were honorable. At once, I realized this is how America should be if it is to continue. I accept this man as my countrymen if that is what he seeks here.

The people of America are far too diverse to maintain the common ground necessary for continuation. Such a diversity has diluted the common interests of our countrymen so much that I fear we are not one. To maintain any notion of a unity we must maintain one common component, whether it be race, religion, or language. The first two were murdered, and so I must deem language the last and only stronghold for the world's epicenter of freedom; only one language must be reign, or say goodbye to our mother America - she will then have been openly slain while her forefathers rest in vain.

I began washing my hands beside them. I went slowly – they a bit faster. The man removed his glasses to douse his face, obviously to refresh it from the complacency of a long drive. The same stagnant appearance was evident on my face, and so we shared something in common above all else that was different. He acknowledged me politely when he understood I was observing his little boy.

The boy's head hardly cleared the counter-top of the sink. He was holding onto his father's leg and fidgeting near the ground all the while. When his father dried his face, the boy said "Dad. You look good without your glasses. But I think…you look better with them." He spoke perfect English. The father didn't answer immediately, so I looked down at him, expecting the boy shy away from me and the thick red beard that was attached to my face, as most children probably would, but I asked anyways "Well, what do you think of *my* glasses?" He hesitated and glanced towards his father who was not willing to give advice, then turned back to me and very articulately said "I think you look very good in your glasses too, sir." I turned to dry my hands smiling, then witnessed a most beautiful event that pleased me best of all; a short series of words that chimed with a simple complexity: "Always be nice to the people. Right dad? It's what you always say."

The father picked the boy up and carried him over his right shoulder smiling to himself. Then he turned towards me and said "goodbye," smiling with a very pleased expression. The boy faced me as they walked out the door and waved, saying "Goodbye, sir, very nice to meet you," with the most perfect manners one could conceive.

CHAPTER 19

It was still night time when I arrived. I leaned against my car and looked at the large, white farm house. It looked much like an old church with its high, wood-siding walls. It was roughly the shape of a T. The clouds weren't hanging low, I was just high in the mountains. They floated faintly above and behind the house, which, by the cause of a powerful moon, were dictated into a similar dimmed shade of white as the house below. Just to the left of this scene, I noticed the silhouette of a row of giant pine trees which served as windbreakers to the house that sat on the face of the mountain. The gaps between their black outlines were filled by the passing grey clouds. The contrast was eerie – especially considering their slow sway to the left and right high at the tops. I then turned my attention to the woods which nearly surrounded me by 360 degrees. There was nothing to see but the first set of silhouettes.

I walked down the hill a piece toward the house and onto the covered side-porch, which was the main entrance. I peered inside the tiny square window panes of the door, to which I saw only darkness. I fumbled with an unfamiliar set of keys at an unfamiliar door knob. When the door swung open I entered into blackness and the smell of old. I looked around and could see nothing. I skimmed the wall with my hand, searching for a light switch. When I didn't find it on the first pass, I started feeling overcome by some off sense of urgency, as if someone was there hiding in the dark.

A very relieving discovery turned on one dim light in the far corner. However relieving it was, the light still left a great deal of dark farmhouse to be discovered. The main room, where I entered, was a large kitchen area connected to a dining room, which was separated only by a wood-stove and brick chimney right in the middle. Everything was wooden in this room; floors, ceilings and walls, including the three white doors which were closed. I opened them one by one: two pantries (one connecting to a back porch), and one large bedroom. There was also a hallway. I avoided it for a while as I pilfered around the room with light. But it couldn't be avoided forever, so I entered into it with hands out in front.

For the first few steps I was guided by the dim light from behind. First appearing on my left was the railing of a stairwell ascending in the opposite direction, whereupon, immediately, a large, black space opened on my right. I scanned the walls with my hands and flipped a light on, whereupon, I found myself looking at the other end of that dark space.

I stood staring straight into the eyes of two black and white painted portraits, separated by a window and its closed curtains in between. The frames were black, in the shape of an oval. On the left was a woman with hair tightly pulled back to a bun with a grim brow hanging low to her eyes. On the right was a stern man with a thick black mustache. Each had pale skin. Neither were handsome. The date said 1809 on each. The two sets of eyes glared at my approach and asked "What are you doing in our home?"

I found a flashlight and headed outside for the cellar door to flip some breakers and turn the water on. Again, I struggled to find the right key. When I entered, it was as I suspected: a terribly dark and spooky cellar. Old tools hung from the ceiling, along with ropes and chains, an old sled, paint cans, rusty fishing poles, canoe paddles, and deteriorated life preservers. I accomplished what I needed and scurried out. When I closed the door behind me, I was alarmed by a sound coming from the woods. An animal was shrieking, and it echoed through the entire holler behind the house and far into the deep forest. Then I heard the coyotes and understood. They were eating something alive; I imagined out of its belly, as the shrilling cry continued to plea for help. Waahhhh! Wahhhh! Wahhhh! I swallowed with sympathy, and having heard enough, retreated into the house to my two companions.

The bulbs were out upstairs, it seemed, so my flashlight guided me. One by one, up the Oak steps I went. It opened to a single hallway with an L at the end, where there stood a room isolated from the rest. In total, there were five closed, white doors with black knobs. I started from one end of the hallway, working my way to the other. It was fairly narrow, so they must have been big rooms, I thought. I made my way to the end of the L, first toward the isolated room. My hand slid across the dusty banister as I walked quietly to the end and made a left, approaching the white door. I could see the first floor below. As the door slowly swung open, not one, but two single beds became visible. They were perfectly made with handcrafted quilts, seemingly untouched. There was a chair, a desk, a dresser, and a closet in the back, which I refrained from opening. The next white door slowly creaked open and I peered inside: a bookshelf full of books, a double bed, perfectly made with an old quilt, and a baby's crib right beside it. I closed it shut and moved to the next. It was a walk-in closet, of course made of wood, but this time, it wasn't so orderly. Half torn wallpaper littered the wooden walls, half removed in some places, torn and what looked to be scratched at in others. Two ancient vacuum cleaners sat on the ground beside a prison mattress that leaned against the back wall. Boxes of old Christmas ornaments were in the corner, with a box of books, several old suits hanging up, and other items of random nature that were scattered about possibly the eeriest room in the house. Behind the next white door were two single beds, each made nicely with old quilts, an empty chest, and a gun rack hanging on the wall with an old .410 gauge shotgun laying in a dusty rest. When I walked into the last room at the other end of the hallway, the light of the rising sun leaked through the window that overlooked the holler where the animal no longer shrieked in horror, but lay in peace. And I rested my body.

CHAPTER 20

The first order of business was removing the portraits. They went in a suitable place - none other than the upstairs closet. The second order was arranging the cabinets; there were **bowls**, and plates, and cups falling out of *all* the cabinets as if I were on a cartoon. I couldn't imagine who would store so much dishware in one place. It took me a day to clean the house. The next day would be fun, so I explored the surrounding woods. The fall foliage was at its height within two weeks of my stay. I soon got into the groove of walking everyday through the woods. Winter would be here in weeks, so I began pulling wood out of the forest every single day. I bought supplies from the store, which was about 20 miles off the mountain in the nearest town. It included a chainsaw, lots of potatoes, three dollar steaks, and a hundred cans of soup. I ate well. I chopped lots of wood. I walked through the forest and studied the animals, sometimes sitting in the same spot for hours. I fished in a small pond down the hill behind the house in front of the holler where the animal cried for help. I soon added jogging, pushups and pull-ups to my routine. I do this everyday as the sun goes down. When I finish, I go inside and make dinner, then read during the night.

I got a cat and named him Stanley. He just looked like a Stan. I watched him grow. He was the biggest of his litter; I chose it that way. He and I have grown big and strong together. I don't baby him; I let him sleep outside with the monsters at night, and he's tougher for it. He practices his skills as much as I do. I watched and studied as he taught himself how to hunt. It didn't take him long at all. To witness this was a great gift from god. The mice no longer bother me. Every night Stanley sits beside me while I read. Before bed I let him out for a night on the town. I worry that he won't return; that his belly will be eaten out by the coyotes like that other animal and I'll hear it from my room. But I think he's a man that knows nature, and accepts it well, so I suppose I will too if that happens. He meows out my window every morning near sunrise and it pisses me off each time. But I still get up, and I'm usually happy I did. He'll disappear sometimes during the day, but if I ever want him, he's never more than a call away. I'll yell three times for him into the woods and he'll come running as fast as he can. He lets me know he's on his way by meowing, and I can hear it a quarter mile down the steep holler. He and I were really strong until just recently. Now were weaker – and different.

There's a small orchard just thirty yards up the hill from the house. Every evening I watch a mother deer bring her two babies up for dinner. They come like clockwork; at 5:15. Stanley and I watch them from the swing on the side porch. They know I'm there. They've always known that I watch them. At first they never took their eye off of me. But soon they became comfortable and stopped checking on me so much and just ate their apples. I started standing from my seat to let them know I could do more than just swing there. Each evening I got a little closer. After about a month, she let me get within twenty feet of her and her babies. I could easily shoot them each evening and be fat and happy. But I won't. We're friends and we've created a bond of trust. I respect it and I respect them. I'll never break it. No matter how hungry I get, I'll never break it. But the rules can change, and I'll shoot her someday - I know it - I don't know why, but I know it. It won't be here at our spot, though – I swear. Soon, though -- I'll do it when the time is right – and in a place that guarantees nothing – where there is no trust for anything nor anyone: The woods - where each animal, including me and Stanley, is at his own risk. I won't do it with a gun. It seems like cheating. I've bought a bow from the pawn shop for eighty bucks. It works well. I'll do it with that. I think I'll be sad. I think about that sadness a bit everyday -- as I'm chopping wood, or painting the house, or walking through the holler; but never mind, I'm going to do it and it's got to be her. I know exactly what she looks like. I know her intimately. I could pick her from a line-up of a hundred deer from these same woods. Of course I do - she's my friend. But I'll be strong like Stanley when the time comes. He can love *and* kill. But mostly he's made for killing.

I have fires every few nights and sit under the stars. Stanley sometimes sits in my lap and watches the fire patiently, as I do. Sometimes he hunts in the woods behind me. It doesn't take him long to come back to the fire and feast beside me. I often watch him eat the belly of something still alive. It bothered me at first, but I've gotten used to it. I'm more animal; that's who I live with, after all. The occasional visit to the store feels weird. I don't even like it.

There are a set of wind chimes in the yard that were given to me as a gift. They hang on the underside of an apple tree at the edge of the yard. They aren't *any little* wind chimes – they're three feet in length, hand crafted tubes that chime a beautiful sound. Behind the yard, where also, I could see from sitting on the porch swing, was an open pasture that went uphill to a knoll. During the day I often take a break right under the chimes and stare out at the other hills and mountains. I often sit flat on my back and look into the perfect blue sky behind the chimes and the tree of which they hang. It feels like a grand return to my baby crib every time.

Thanksgiving came and I spent it alone. But I shot me a big fat turkey with that shotgun, which made me happy. I'm not much for cooking, but if I set out to do it right, I ain't half bad. I sat there alone with my big table of food and hardly recognized I was alone. Stan ate the other half of the turkey. I ate fast like it was any other meal. Then I cleaned up fast like it was any other meal.

When winter came knocking at my front door it wouldn't leave. As each fresh layer of snow piled on the previous, it never got easier for me to trample on nature's plentiful artwork. I was reluctant to put my ugly tracks through it each and every time. I got buried-in good, and it got damn cold out here. But I stayed strong and warm and never flinched a-once from it. This existence has turned the clock back for me: I feel younger, stronger, and happier - my old knee and back pains from sports are gone, vanished; my hair-line even grown back after receding. No, the winter didn't get me down at all. I didn't stay cooped-up inside, either. I went out. I walked through that snow, and consumed all the sunshine I could.

The woods are much quieter in the winter, but I stirred them up. And I chopped, and I ate, and I read. I burned hot fires of Cherry - the sweetest aroma of all the trees. If a doctor diagnosed me with cancer, this is where I would go, *this* how I would live – not because I like it so much, but because it's the medicine I believe in. I'd come back to this place and be strong like I am now. I'd run everyday up the mountain, beating the piss out of body – making my heart pump so much fresh blood that it flushed any illness out; and I would eat, and I would chop, and read, and sleep; be more animal.

I've been home once, for Christmas, since living here. I went to a Methodist Church service with my family just like any other year, and I enjoyed it well. But mostly I remember is this: one day I was in a metered parking lot in West Chester, Pennsylvania at 8 a.m. I was the only car in the lot, which was **completely covered by snow**. I put my quarters in the meter and went on my business. When I returned an hour later, a parking ticket awaited me under the driver's side wiper: *'parking outside of designated lane'* it said. Let me remind you, no lanes were visible whatsoever and I still had fifteen minutes left on the meter. I took it straight to the court and wrote an appeal. They denied it faster than I could write it out. I tried to contact several other people who had the power to make our society exponentially better, instead, they *all* chose to ignore me and allowed the menace we've created to penetrate our mother liberty. I didn't pay it for a while out of sheer resentment, but finally gave-in when the third ticket for $150 bucks arrived in the mail with a warrant out for my arrest. I feel like a woman in a domestic abuse situation. I love my country and I'll never leave her, but she holds me down and beats me. Returning to the farmhouse was more justified than ever.

I had a new Christmas gift with me when I returned. I was deep in the holler behind the house. I'd been sitting still, watching and waiting for hours - with my stinging toes sunk deep in the snow – deep inside my thick boot; but I was hungry and it didn't matter at all. It was dead quiet - all except for the occasional gust that cut through and *it* was even a quaint sound, is if the wind itself didn't care for being cold. I was halfway down a hill, hunkered behind a pile of brush, in hiding. The wind wasn't blowing uphill, so I knew my scent wouldn't get carried up, which means, they'd stumble onto me unexpectedly from above. Without their scent, we're on the same playing field.

I was in her home and I identified her right away when she showed. The white triangle on her throat is unmistakable. None were as pretty as her – not even close. Her coat was a light brown, thick, and healthy. I peered at her through the limbs of my cover like a savage. She was smart – r*eal smart*, so I was careful not to disturb her. The longer I stalked, the more intense my heartbeat grew. Imagine for a moment the sound of Amazon hunters beating on their drums before a hunt. Imagine fifty of them in face paint angrily stomping around a big fire, resembling wild beasts - the longer it goes on, the more intense it gets: that was the type of rhythm that overtook me right then and there. She sifted through the snow, then raised her head to watch and look, then sifted and looked again repeatedly – just as she did when we first met, only this time she sensed something different than trust; only this time, those same drums beat intensely in each of us. I waited for her to get closer. I waited, then did more waiting. I wanted it like that: personal. I had a scope that could hit a penny a mile away, but I wanted it close so it was fair. And she was doing it, too; gradually sifting her way toward me; in and out of trees, often blending in with the background and disappearing. Several times I'd frantically thought I lost her, but remained patient, and each time, somewhere off in the brown thicket I would catch her head lifting up behind a tree or behind some brush, chewing just like she did on my apples. I would have eaten those apples, darn it. That's what I told myself, at least - that I was getting my property back. But when she came within the same distance of the apple trees to the porch – the distance I was so familiar with seeing her at – I kept seeing the face of an old friend, and so a dilemma arose in my head. Would I break the agreement to myself not to use a gun? What would that make me? Should one use reason to alter an agreement he's previously established with himself?

She always seemed to be protected by a tree. But as she came closer, that would change. I slowly moved the gun into position. Oh, how beautiful, I thought, when she came just on the other side of my brush pile. Her chest was now fully exposed to me yet all I could seem to do was observe her in awe. She still sifted casually through the snow. But the big moment arrived much faster than I would have preferred when she raised her head in one quick jolt and spotted me through the debris. She turned her head square at me, looking with two piercing eyes of friendship. She knew it was me right away; I know she knew.

CHAPTER 21

This morning I woke up to the sun peeking through my window and the sound of Stanley's voice at the door. I made two eggs, two slices of bacon, two pieces of toast, then threw-in a large piece of dark chocolate before I headed out the door. When I was a little boy I couldn't wait to get out that door and play, and I still can't. You would hardly believe the beauty outside if I told you. It's late in the spring time now. The woods are covered in red, white, blue, and purple, flowers; *all* colors. Sure, I'd like to tell you all about winter; hell, I would have liked to tell you about a lot of other things, but I reckon I'd better wrap this thing up – we've been sitting here so long the sun's going down on us.

The hay now swayed wildly with the wind. After my breakfast I grabbed a fishing pole and walked down the holler where a fresh mountain stream runs through, to which I caught some nibbles of several trout too small for my hook and came home with a smile. I put the pole away and walked up to the wind chimes. Taking care of life's utensil, I stretched my legs in the grass and did pull-ups on one of the apple trees. Then I headed off for a short jog.

Like I said, the field here descends at my feet and it meets the forest line about 200 yards down hill, and thereafter, the forest continues on for about a hundred miles. The field is encompassed by this forest on all sides. It's hidden, in fact, from anyone knowing of it at all. Its farmers have long passed. But maybe they sat in this same spot one day long ago, looking out as I am now. The meeting of two mountains is at the bottom of this field and through a mile of woods straight down. The face of that other mountain is in plane sight to me. It, too, has a field, which is plainly visible from where I sit. But it rather should be called a pasture, for there are live sheep on it, by which our exact distance just nearly permits my eyes to articulate the difference between head and body of the sheep that are scattered about.

While I was jogging I realized how all that power and strength gained though fall and winter had begun to dissipate. I was weaker. When I came back from that run, don't ask how, but by and by, I've come across a woman this spring, and she was waiting for me inside. All of those **bowls** in the house and none of them would hold a decent amount of cereal; they were all so small and shallow. All winter, I agonized with cans of soup overflowing my bowls. Very recently, I struck some luck in the back of a cabinet and found a big **bowl** that would hold any damn can of soup I wished. I like a big bowl, so I put this one in the rotation.

When I walked in the door, I noticed that very bowl I speak of was out of its place. It sat in the middle of the dinner table. 'That's odd,' I thought to myself. Her and I passed one another in the hallway and walked by without a word. She gave me a stern look. Something was up, but I didn't pay any mind - I was busy doing things. When I returned to the kitchen she stood next to the bowl and pointed at it, saying:

'Where did that bowl come from?'

To which I replied 'Hell if I know,' and walked away.

The truth was, I suppose I knew exactly where the bowl came from, but what cabinet it came from didn't matter and surely wasn't worth an explanation to *anyone* who asked. So I continued on my business, completely ignoring the silly question. Ten, fifteen, forty minutes later, I don't know, I passed by her again in one of the rooms downstairs, and she gave me another funny look. She said very aggressively:

'Why did you lie to me about that bowl?'

I was amazed at the persistence. After a second serious inquiry of the bowl's origins, I scanned for ideas about what might be going on until I thought I knew what she was poking at. I'll admit to being a scoundrel once or twice in my day, but certainly not to this one. She'd lost her mind if she was thinking what I thought she was thinking. Therefore, I wasn't interested in entertaining such a discussion, which is why my reply exacerbated the situation terribly, when it could have properly dissolved it.

'I don't know where that *damned* **bowl** came from. What are you gettin' at anyways?'

'You're lying! I know it.'

I stomped away in disbelief and went to sharpen my chainsaw and tinker with some other things. When I came back in, I was completely ignored; not even looked at. And that was fine by me – she'd get over it. We didn't talk for hours - over a **bowl**.

Finally the pressure of silence started pecking at me so much that I had to break it. My first attempt was:

'What's for dinner, baby?'

That didn't work at all, so we went even longer without speaking. I tinkered with some more stuff outside, but the situation inside still bothered me. I went back inside and she passed me somewhere again without even a look.

'The bowl came from the cabinet to the left of the coffee maker, in the back, on the very top shelf! Happy?' I yelled clear from a different room.

I probably could have just said that from the beginning, but sometimes I can't bring myself to answer such questions. Later, I was informed that specific bowl is used for holding desert dishes like rice pudding. Is it coming together now?

'Well how come I've washed every bowl in this house and I've never seen that one!?'

I noticed the sound of a fly pestering the ceiling, which propagated the vexing atmosphere of the room. This irony is all I was really thinking about.

'Because you *clearly* haven't washed every bowl!' I yelled

'Do you think I'm too sensitive for you?'

Absolutely perplexed at such a tactic, I bought time by repeating it extra slowly:

'*Do I think you're too sensitive for me*? No baby, you're not too sensitive for me' I said, smoothing things over to con my way back to peace and quiet.

I walked toward her with my arms out and we enjoyed a brief hug. But I couldn't just keep my mouth shut and said:

'But you really are sensitive sometimes, and you need to understand that so you can fix it.'

'You make me that way! You're so short with me and grouchy!'

And I'll admit, this was true, but it was all I could do to get a breath of fresh air and out of each other's face.

'Like the other day . . .' she continued on.

And this resulted in another argument of a good portion of ten minutes, to which ended with another hour or two of angry, tense silence. All I remember is yelling something like: 'What were my exact words? You tell me!!' - and her replying with a skewed order of my words. It was a mess. Meanwhile, a beautiful day was occurring outside. My final question before I stormed out the door and walked to the place where I now sit was:

'Well. What's for dinner? Are you cooking dinner? *I'll* make it if you don't want.'

'No. I'm making it' she put her foot down with frustration.
'Well, making what!?'
'Venison! The stuff you have in the freezer! Is that *okay*?'
'Fine!'

I walked out the door, which led me on a walk to where I now sit.

CHAPTER 22

Rolling over to my side, I feel through the soothing ground with my hands. I embrace its comfort by planting my face into the grass with arms and legs spread wide, clinging not just onto that surface, but onto the entire earth, by wrapping my fingers around many blades of grass to prevent the massive rotation from tossing me into space, as I ride, round and round. Like a child, there's a hidden smile beneath. The weight of my heavy body puts pressure on my rib cage and my heartbeat drives into the hard ground as the energy from deep within the hot core pumps right back with it; one in the same.

I think of the people – all of them – my brothers and sisters. They have changed in the recent years, and I get a funny feeling from it. They exhibit anxious behavior; they exist in a state of rush, hurrying to accomplish the last-minute task of living. But it seems to be in a frantic, instinctual manner – like the animals before an approaching tidal wave – all very unconsciously. But I don't worry; it's only a sign of natural things ahead.

Looking up and out, I'm witness to the sun setting on the brim of that mountain, just beyond the white dots of sheep. I think back to those who made me believe the sun rests complacent and still, and only we, the earth, move around it; and I'm obliged to recollect those who once believed the world was flat. And amongst such transformational properties, in one instant moment of time, I'm helplessly overwhelmed in thought: for the sheep, who, away with the light, can no longer distinguish my head and body, if they ever could, also fade with the light, and at once, I'm struck by that always present and omnipotent truth – a scary and inescapable truth – of the speck that I really am: at once frightening; at twice funny. Just funny.

ACKNOWLEDGEMENTS

To the family, friends, and teachers of my past and present: you influenced my writing and shaped my ideas; I thank you. To all the truckers, the farmers, and people of Europe - you are my story. And to the friendly people of West Virginia: the beauty of your forests and mountains were my home while I composed this book.

My greatest appreciation to the original writer of <u>A Letter to End a Love Affair</u>, my dear friend and great Estonia writer, actor, translator: Edvin Aedma.

-Jesse Clay Antoine